Study Guide to Accompany Cavanaugh's

Adult Development and Aging

SECOND EDITION

BRADLEY J. CASKEY

University of Wisconsin—River Falls

I(T)P ™ The trademark ITP is used under license.

Brooks/Cole Publishing Company
A Division of Wadsworth, Inc.

Printed in the United States of America

10 9 8 7 6 5 4 3

Cover Art: David Hockney: *Mt. Fuji and Flowers,* 1972. Acrylic on canvas, 60 x 48 in. The Metropolitan Museum of Art, Purchase. Mrs. Arthur Hays Sulzberger Gift, 1972. (1972.128) © David Hockney.

ISBN 0-534-17253-9

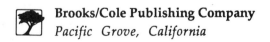**Brooks/Cole Publishing Company**
Pacific Grove, California

CONTENTS

PREFACE

Since you are reading this, I can assume that you are currently enrolled in a course on Adult Development and Aging and your teacher has wisely selected John Cavanaugh's **Adult Development and Aging (2nd Ed.)** text. I think that you will like the Cavanaugh text. In reviewing it for the preparation of this study guide, I found it to be informative and highly readable.

The primary purpose of this preface is to provide you with some guidance on using this study guide most effectively. As you will see, I have divided chapters in the study guide into five sections, each with a unique purpose. The **PREVIEW** section is to be used **prior** to reading the Cavanaugh text. The goal of this section is to guide you through the most important issues and concepts discussed in each chapter. Begin by carefully reading the **Focus Questions**. Then take a quick look at the **Chapter Outline**. Finally, read the corresponding textbook chapter with the focus questions in mind.

The **REVIEW** section is designed to be completed **after** you have read the text chapter. It contains several "self-test" sections designed to assess your level of comprehension and retention of the text material. The **Terms to Know** section is used to strengthen your vocabulary for critical concepts. The **True/False, Fill-in-the-Blank(s)** and **Multiple Choice** sections assess your knowledge for and comprehension of specific ideas or information.

The **SHORT ANSWER ESSAY** section also is designed to be completed **after** you have read the textbook chapter. In this section, I have identified major research or theoretical items that do not lend themselves well to multiple-choice, fill-in-the-blank or true/false formats. Answers to the essay items (with a text page reference) are found after the last essay question. It is critical to keep in mind, however, that these are **my** suggested answers and it is likely that the format of your answers will not match my suggestions. I tend to use a very structured style and like to create lists (with examples) whenever possible. You may have a preference for a more detailed answer and that is perfectly fine. The key in this section is to try and match the **content** of the suggested answer, not the format!

One goal of education is to assist students in becoming more critical thinkers and one aspect of critical thinking involves reflecting on the implications of course material beyond the classroom. The **AFTER THE FACTS** section is designed to encourage you to think about issues discussed in the text and speculate on your solutions or opinions concerning each issue. As you will see, answers to the **AFTER THE FACTS** items are highly subjective and, as a result, are intended to be answered "in your head," not on paper.

The **ANSWERS** section provides immediate feedback as to the accuracy of your responses to the **REVIEW** section items. It also identifies the pages from which the answer was derived. I have located this information at the end of each chapter so you will not have to search for it.

As stated earlier, I have designed this study guide to enhance your comprehension and retention of the material presented in the Cavanaugh text. I believe that if you follow the suggestions made in this preface, take the time to read the text, and answer the **REVIEW** and **SHORT ANSWER ESSAY** items, you will find the guide to be a truly effective learning aid.

I hope you find the guide useful. Also, good luck and have a great class!

ACKNOWLEDGMENTS

I wish to thank Lynda (my wife) for the emotional and technical support she provided during the preparation of this study guide. I could not have done it without her. I also wish to thank Alex (my daughter) for encouraging me to take on this job. Additional thanks go to Kenneth King (Senior Editor) for getting me started, Dr. Rik Seefeldt (colleague and friend) for suggestions made during the process, and the entire Brooks/Cole editing team. Finally, special thanks to Julie Davis (Assistant Editor) for getting me through my first manuscript!

CHAPTER 1
INTRODUCTION TO ADULT DEVELOPMENT
AND AGING

I. PREVIEW

Focus Questions

☞ **Is aging influenced more by heredity or by environmental factors?**
(Focus on: The Nature-Nurture Controversy)

☞ **How stable is development in adulthood?**
(Focus on: The Continuity-Discontinuity Controversy)

☞ **What different basic assumptions are made by the three dominant world models of development?**
(Focus on: Moving from Issues to Models)

☞ **What is the biopsychosocial approach to aging?**
(Focus on: The Biopsychosocial Model)

☞ **What are the strengths/weaknesses of cross-sectional, longitudinal, time-lag, and sequential designs?**
(Focus on: Developmental Research Designs)

☞ **Are there any advantages to naturalistic versus experimental approaches to research?**
(Focus on: Approaches to Doing Research)

1

Chapter 1: INTRODUCTION

Chapter Outline

Chapter 1: INTRODUCTION

II. REVIEW

Terms to Know
Write your own brief definition for each of the following terms.

Age Effects:

Ageism:

Biological Age:

Biopsychosocial Model:

Chronological Age:

Cohort Effects:

Contextual Model:

Continuity-Discontinuity Controversy:

Correlational Technique:

Cross-Sectional Design:

Experiment:

Gerontology:

Longitudinal Design:

Mechanistic Model:

Naturalistic Inquiry:

Chapter 1: INTRODUCTION

Nature-Nurture Controversy:

Nonnormative Influences:

Normative Age-Graded Influences:

Normative History-Graded Influences:

Organismic Model:

Psychological Age:

Qualitative Change:

Quantitative Change:

Reliability:

Sequential Designs:

Social Age:

Social Clock:

Time-Lag Design:

Time-of-Measurement Effects:

Validity:

True/False Questions

___ 1. The increase in the number of elderly people will create new jobs for the young.

___ 2. The organismic model assumes that the whole is equal to the sum of its parts.

___ 3. The age-65 retirement criteria is an example of a social time event.

___ 4. Data suggests that chronic illnesses have little impact on personal development.

___ 5. Age causes most developmental changes.

___ 6. Chronological age is a good example of a surrogate variable.

___ 7. Winning the lottery is a nonnormative life event.

___ 8. Cross-sectional designs often paint a bleak picture of aging.

___ 9. A valid measure assesses a variable in a consistent manner.

___ 10. Representativeness helps ensure generalization of data to the entire population.

Fill-in-the-Blank(s) Questions

1. _____ is the study of aging from young adulthood through old age.

2. Discrimination against older people is called _____.

3. If you study the amount that a characteristic changes with development, you are focusing on _____ change. If, however, you assess the development of a new ability, you are investigating _____ changes.

4. The mechanistic model uses a(n) _____ as the best metaphor for understanding humans.

5. Family membership is a(n) _____ factor that might influence adult behaviors.

6. _____ aging refers to normal, disease-free development in adulthood.

7. Intelligence and memory abilities are examples of your
   _____ age.
8. A _____ group is any collection of people having
   some common experience.
9. When subjects begin but do not finish a longitudinal task, there may
   be a problem with _____. For example, we can end
   up with _____ if only high-scoring subjects are left
   at the end of the study.
10. Schaie called his combination of cross-sequential and longitudinal
    sequential designs the _____ because it addressed
    most of the major problems associated with developmental research.

Multiple Choice Questions

1. The belief that old people are _____ is an example of
   ageism.
   A. incompetent   C. asexual
   B. decrepit   D. all of the above

2. _____ is an example of a nurture-based influence.
   A. Having Down syndrome (as the result of possessing an extra
      21st chromosome)
   B. Having lived with a person with AIDS
   C. Inheriting Huntington's disease
   D. all of the above

3. Quantitative changes in behavior are
   A. the main focus of the Piagetian and Eriksonian models of human
      development.
   B. critical to the discontinuity position of development.
   C. may reflect age differences in responding.
   D. all of the above

4. Most researchers interested in adult development and aging take
   a(n)_____ approach to the nature-nurture issue.
   A. nature only
   B. nurture only
   C. interactionist (both nature and nurture)

5. Individuals with a(n) _____ orientation would focus
   exclusively on environmental factors to explain the development
   of love and attraction.
   A. humanistic   C. organismic
   B. mechanistic   D. contextual

6. The _____ world model believes strongly in the
   multidirectionality of development.
   A. humanistic   C. organismic
   B. mechanistic   D. contextual

7. Chronological age is best associated with _____ time.
   A. life   C. social
   B. historical   D. maintenance

8. Desert Storm and "the Reagan Era" are examples of _____ time.
   A. life   C. social
   B. historical   D. maintenance

9. The concept of emergence is best associated with the statement
   A. "All men are created equal."
   B. "You only go around once in life."
   C. "The whole is greater than the sum of its parts."
   D. "Often life is not worth living."

10. _____ is an intrapersonal factor.
    A. Memory   C. Intelligence
    B. Personality   D. all of the above

11. Loss of memory from Alzheimer's disease is a good example of
    A. primary aging.   C. secondary aging.
    B. initial aging.   D. tertiary aging.

12. _____ aging involves a rapid loss that occurs just before death.
    A. Primary   C. Secondary
    B. Initial   D. Tertiary

13. Growing gray hair is
    A. caused by time.   C. dependent on time.
    B. irrelevant to time.   D. negatively related to time.

14. Mary is 60 years old, drives a Corvette, and has a teenage daughter. She would be considered to have a young
    A. chronological age.   C. biological age.
    B. social age.   D. psychological age.

15. The developmentally _____ approach seeks to understand how change occurs and what characterizes change.
    A. dynamic   C. different
    B. static   D. centric

16. The "sexual revolution" in the 1960s is an example of a
    A. normative age-graded event.
    B. normative history-graded event.
    C. normative individual-graded event.
    D. nonnormative event.

17. A(n) _____ effect is due to the unique experiences of a specific group of people.
    A. age   C. nonstandard
    B. cohort   D. nonnormative

18. Practice effects are a major problem with _____ designs.
   A. longitudinal   C. time-lag
   B. cross-sectional   D. all of the above

19. Age changes are studied most effectively using a _____ design.
   A. longitudinal   C. time-lag
   B. cross-sectional   D. all of the above

20. A _____ design measures at different times, different groups of subjects who are the same age.
   A. longitudinal   C. time-lag
   B. cross-sectional   D. all of the above

21. A _____ design combines two or more cross-sectional designs.
   A. longitudinal   C. time-lag
   B. cross-sequential   D. longitudinal sequential

22. Which of the following is **not** an adequate measurement concern?
   A. representativeness   C. validity
   B. reliability   D. all are adequate concerns

23. Experiments
   A. involve the manipulation of a variable.
   B. often use age as an independent variable.
   C. always utilize reliable assessment devices.
   D. all of the above

24. Correlational studies
   A. are effective with variables that can't be manipulated.
   B. can provide important information about the strength of relationships between variables.
   C. can't provide information concerning causation.
   D. all of the above

III. SHORT-ANSWER ESSAY (QUESTIONS AND ANSWERS)

Questions

1. Describe the nature-nurture controversy.

2. What is the basic premise of the continuity-discontinuity controversy?

3. Differentiate between the mechanistic, organismic, and contextual models of human development.

4. How are the concepts of life time, social time, and historical time different?

5. What are the components of the biopsychosocial model?

6. Which definitions of age have been considered in the biopsychosocial model?

7. Define and provide an example of a normative age-graded event, a normative history-graded event, and a nonnormative event.

8. Differentiate between age, cohort, and time-of-measurement effects.

9. Identify and define the basic developmental research designs.

10. What are advantages and disadvantages of experimental and correlational techniques?

Answers

1. The nature-nurture controversy involves an attempt to discover the <u>cause</u> of developmental change. Theorists taking a strong nature position argue that developmental change is best explained by inherited biological factors. Nurture theorists argue that human development occurs because of experience. Most developmental theorists today take an "interactionist" approach emphasizing the importance of the interaction between heredity and the environment. (p. 5-6)

2. The focus of the continuity-discontinuity controversy is on the <u>nature</u> of change across the lifespan. Continuity theorists tend to view change as quantitative (i.e., you get more or less of the same basic process), whereas discontinuity theorists see change best described in qualitative terms (i.e., often in "stages" in which you acquire new and differing processes). (p. 6-7)

3. Mechanists tend to view development as quantitative and nurture-influenced. These theorists use a machine as the basic metaphor for humans. Organismic model theorists see development as involving qualitative changes (stage shifts) with a specific goal or endpoint to development. The basic metaphor is a biological organism whose whole is greater than the sum of its parts. Contextualists view life in terms of historic events. They tend to see change as multidirectional and are interested in complex nature-nurture interaction explanations for change. (p. 8-9)

4. Life time refers to chronological age. Social time reflects age-appropriate behaviors that are determined by society (e.g., retirement at age 65). Historical time is a global term concerning prevailing political, economic, and environmental events that differ with each generation (e.g., the AIDS epidemic or the recession of 1991-92). (p. 11)

5. The biopsychosocial model has four main components. Interpersonal factors involve relationship skills. Intrapersonal factors include both set biological variables (e.g., age and sex) and psychological types (e.g., memory and intelligence). Biological and physical factors include any chronic illness or other types of functional incapacity. Finally, life-cycle factors look at how chronological age differences may result in different reactions (e.g., a 15-year-old and a 55-year-old might react differently to the same event). (p. 12-14)

6. Biological age, which is assessed by the functioning of various life-limiting organ systems. Social age, which involves specific roles adopted by a person in a given culture at a given age to conform to expectations. Psychological age, which refers to the ability to adapt to environmental variation. (p. 16-17)

7. Normative age-graded events are biological and environmental events highly related to age (e.g., ability to drive, vote, have children). Normative history-graded events are cultural experiences common to most people in a culture (e.g., the 1960s political assassinations, 1970s disco). A nonnormative event is experienced by a particular individual but few others (e.g., surviving a plane crash or winning the lottery). (p. 19)

8. Age effects focus on basic changes that have occurred within a person with the passage of time. Cohort effects reflect group effects caused by unique social, environmental, or biological events common to a large percentage of a population. Time-of-measurement effects focus on the influence of the current social, cultural, and biological environment on the reactions of subjects. (p. 20-21)

9. Cross-sectional design compares different groups of people at the same time. Longitudinal design compares the same people at different times. Time-lag design measures groups of people of the same age at different times. Cross-sequential design combines two or more cross-sectional designs. Longitudinal sequential design combines two or more longitudinal designs. Schaie's "most efficient design," combines all of the fore-mentioned techniques. (p. 21-26)

10. Experimental designs allow for the determination of cause through the manipulation of variables often at the expense of ecological validity (i.e., are conducted often in artificial situations). Correlations allow one to assess the relationship between variables that are difficult to manipulate (e.g., drinking and prenatal trauma); however, correlational data cannot be used to assess causation. (p. 27-28)

IV. AFTER THE FACTS

1. What kinds of normative history-graded events are taking place today? How might you be affected by such social events?

2. What interpersonal, intrapersonal, and biological factors do you see as having had a great impact on your current self? What future time-related events might have an impact?

3. What advantages are there to conceptualizing "age" in numerous ways (i.e., chronological, biological, psychological)? How might your knowledge of the existence of these different "types of age" affect your answer to the question "What is your age?"

4. Think about the ideas that you have concerning adult development and aging. Having just reviewed information on research methods, can you identify any "truths" that you hold that might be based on poorly designed studies or observations?

V. REVIEW ANSWERS

Terms to Know
Check the Key Terms section for Chapter 1 (p. 32-33)

True/False Answers
1. True (p.4)	6. True (p.18)
2. False (p.8)	7. True (p.19)
3. True (p.11)	8. True (p.22)
4. False (p.14)	9. False (p.27)
5. False (p.16)	10. True (p.26)

Fill-in-the-Blank(s) Answers
1. Gerontology (p. 4)
2. ageism (p. 4)
3. quantitative (p. 7); qualitative (p. 7)
4. machine (p. 8)
5. interpersonal (p. 12)
6. Primary (p. 16)
7. psychological (p. 17)
8. cohort (p. 20)
9. participant dropout (p. 23); positive selective survival (p. 23)
10. "most efficient design" (p. 26)

Multiple Choice Answers
1. D (p.4)	9. C (p.11)	17. B (p.20-21)
2. B (p.7)	10. D (p.13)	18. A (p.23)
3. C (p.7)	11. C (p.16)	19. A (p.21-23)
4. C (p.8)	12. D (p.16)	20. C (p.23)
5. B (p.8)	13. C (p.16)	21. B (p.24)
6. D (p.9)	14. B (p.17)	22. A (p.26-27)
7. A (p.11)	15. A (p.18)	23. A (p.27-28)
8. B (p.11)	16. B (p.19)	24. D (p.28)

CHAPTER 2
DIVERSITY

I. PREVIEW

Focus Questions

☞ **How is our current population distributed (with respect to age, race, gender)?**
(Focus on: The Demographics of Aging)

☞ **What future demographic trends are anticipated?**
(Focus on: The Demographics of Aging)

☞ **In what ways does our status change as we age?**
(Focus on: Status, Role, and Gender)

☞ **What kind of "unwritten" societal rules might affect the way your behavior might change as you age?**
(Focus on: Age Stratification)

☞ **How does ethnic status impact aging?**
(Focus on: Ethnicity and Age)

☞ **Do all cultures treat adults in the same way?**
(Focus on: Patterns of Aging Across Cultures)

Chapter 2: DIVERSITY

Chapter Outline

II. REVIEW

Terms to Know
Write your own brief definition for each of the following terms.

Acculturation:

Age Norms:

Age Stratification Model:

Age-Set Systems:

Anticipatory Socialization:

Double Jeopardy:

Egalitarian Societies:

Ethnic Group:

Ethnic Identity:

Ethnogerontology:

Intergenerational Conflict:

Modernization Theory:

Ranked Horticultural Societies:

Societal Significance:

Chapter 2: DIVERSITY

True/False Questions

___ 1. The use of age 65 to define the lower limits of "old-age" is linked to Hippocrates' ancient notion of the "lifespan."

___ 2. Between 2010 and 2030 it is estimated that the elderly population of the U.S. will increase by 25 million.

___ 3. In the U.S. women have always outnumbered men.

___ 4. About 20 percent of the world's societies currently practice gericide (killing of the elderly).

___ 5. Most researchers agree that women age with less difficulty than men.

___ 6. Projects indicate that the societal significance for the elderly population will increase significantly in the next 20 years.

___ 7. Bastida's research on Hispanics found that they held strong age related beliefs concerning dress, courtship, and ability to discuss sexual behavior.

___ 8. In Confucianism, personhood ends with physical death.

___ 9. Egalitarian societies are run by consensus.

___ 10. The Japanese continue to revere and value highly the elderly in their society.

Fill-in-the-Blank(s) Questions

1. The elderly population of third world nations is expected to _____ in the next 50 years.

2. The process of examining how successive birth cohorts move across time is called a(n) _____.

3. A cohort group's degree of control over other cohorts is referred to as their _____.

4. Teaching people how they should expect to act after they become parents is an example of the broader process of _____, which prepares people for age related changes in status or roles.

5. Changing one's expectations after the acquisition of a new role involves _____.

6. A(n) _____ studies the effects of race and culture on aging.
7. Talley and Kaplan originally used the term _____ to describe the situation of being old and _____.
8. The social phenomena that result when two or more cultures interact is called _____.
9. _____ theory argues that devaluation of the elderly will always occur in technologically based societies.
10. A culture in which group membership is based on common age operates with a(n) _____ system.

Multiple Choice Questions

1. _____ is **not** a population demographic characteristic.
   A. Your IQ score
   B. The number of elderly married persons
   C. The number of Asian Americans living in Texas
   D. all are population demographics

2. Approximately _____ of the current U.S. population turned 65 after 1975.
   A. 20%   C. 60%
   B. 40%   D. 80%

3. There are approximately _____ older adults in the U.S. today.
   A. 300,000   C. 30,000,000
   B. 3,000,000   D. 300,000,000

4. In the near future, the number of elderly _____ persons is expected to increase significantly.
   A. Native-American   C. Hispanic
   B. African-American   D. all of the above

5. In the U.S. in the past 20 years, the number of elderly
   _____ has shown the fastest increase.
   A. Native-Americans   C. Hispanics
   B. African-Americans   D. whites

6. According to Rosow's Structural Perspective, old age in the U.S.
   represents status without
   A. a role.   C. relationships.
   B. an economic advantage.   D. stability.

7. Which is **not** a basic premise of the Interactionist Perspective?
   A. We often choose the particular status we occupy.
   B. All roles have narrowly defined behavioral expectations.
   C. We often choose the specific role we act out.
   D. People often create informal roles of personal interest.

8. The process of setting up age related rights, roles, and privileges is
   central to the concept of age
   A. decentration.   C. infiltration.
   B. stratification.   D. oneness.

9. Which statement describes the concept of age grades?
   A. "Grandpa, act your age."
   B. "Retired people don't have to work."
   C. "Married women in their 30s should have children."
   D. all of the above

10. In most cultures, people of higher stratification
    A. have great impact on those below them in status.
    B. are very old.
    C. are of moderate socioeconomic status.
    D. all of the above

11. In the U.S., the strongest age norms are found for _____ issues.
    A. political activity
    B. family
    C. friendship
    D. religious

12. The largest predicted drop in societal significance in the elderly is found when you focus on
    A. relative cohort size.
    B. family involvement.
    C. work involvement.
    D. all of the above

13. _____ is an example of a common adult socialization event.
    A. Losing a job
    B. Parenting
    C. Retirement
    D. all of the above

14. According to Schemerhorn, _____ do not qualify as an ethnic group.
    A. Hispanics
    B. Mexicans
    C. Cubans
    D. Germans

15. According to Helzberg, being Irish qualifies as being
    A. a minority group.
    B. an ethnic group.
    C. both a minority and an ethnic group.
    D. neither a minority nor an ethnic group.

16. Ethnicity
    A. may play a role in adult development.
    B. has several definitions.
    C. is often confounded with other factors leading to problems in predictability.
    D. all of the above

Chapter 2: DIVERSITY

17. African-American women tend to
    A. have very narrow definitions of kinship relationships.
    B. focus heavily on chronological age as predicting behavior.
    C. value wisdom over possessions.
    D. all of the above

18. Research on older Korean immigrants living in the New York City area indicated that almost two thirds
    A. had above average incomes.
    B. could not read or speak English.
    C. wanted to return to Korea.
    D. seldom took advantage of available social services.

19. Research on acculturation has shown all of the following **except**:
    A. It has led to health problems in Mexican Americans.
    B. Older Korean immigrants were more alienated than younger Korean immigrants.
    C. First-generation immigrants are seldom affected by the new culture.
    D. Canada has dealt with the issue of second-language support differently than has the U.S.

20. Most cultures that minimize the importance of "stages" in life tend to
    A. be very small in size.
    B. lack personal property ownership.
    C. have fluid social relationships.
    D. all of the above

21. Which statement concerning rituals is **false**?
    A. Thanksgiving is a ritual.
    B. Rituals often involve a specific form of dress.
    C. Rituals create feelings of discontinuity among generations.
    D. Rituals are often overseen by persons with perceived life experiences and wisdom.

22. Ranked horticultural societies
    A. have a clear ranking system including a chief or "big men."
    B. tend to "share the wealth" among all its members.
    C. rely heavily on age as a determinant of status.
    D. all of the above

23. Research on age, gender, and power has shown that
    A. women never have more power than men.
    B. younger women tend to have more power than older women.
    C. older men's power is based most often on physical strength.
    D. childbearing status may play a role in determining power for women.

24. Intergenerational conflicts are found
    A. only in egalitarian societies.
    B. only in ranked horticultural societies.
    C. only in western societies.
    D. in all cultures.

III. SHORT-ANSWER ESSAY (QUESTIONS AND ANSWERS)

Questions

1. What percentage of the current U.S. population is over age 65? How has this number changed since 1900? What will this number be by 2030?

2. What trends in aging demographics are expected with regard to ethnic groups and gender distributions?

3. What is the basic premise of Rosow's Structuralist Perspective of Aging? What are the two main problems with his arguments?

4. List reasons why most researchers believe that women age with less difficulty than men?

5. Uhlenberg stated that influence and power are affected by three factors. Describe them.

6. What are some examples of anticipatory socialization?

7. Differentiate between Schermerhorn and Holzberg's definitions of ethnicity.

8. How was the term double jeopardy used in the chapter? What conclusions were drawn concerning the reality of this problem?

9. What were the major findings of Bastida's study on age-related norms in a Hispanic population?

10. What were the key elements of Luborsky and Rubinstein's research on the importance of ethnic identity?

11. What are some of the determinants of status found in other cultures but not used in the U.S.?

12. Is the U.S. closer to an egalitarian or ranked horticultural society?

13. How would you react to the statement that Asians hold a powerful reverence for their elderly?

Answers

1. Currently about 12 percent of Americans are over age 65. This is up from about 4 percent in 1900, but significantly less than the 17 percent estimated for 2030. (p. 37)

2. Tremendous growth is expected in the number of elderly African-Americans, Hispanics, Asian/Pacific Islanders, and Native-Americans. Also, the number of elderly women is expected to continue to exceed that of men. (p. 39-40)

3. Rosow's Structuralist Perspective Model of Sociological Theory emphasizes the importance of status (formal rights and privileges denoted by a society) versus roles (a set of behavioral rights or duties). Rosow says that in the U.S. the elderly represent a group with status but no roles. He further proposes that because of this situation, the elderly lose self-concept and cannot meet the demands of society. Research, however, has shown that self-concept in the elderly is often unaffected by loss of identity and many elderly persons successfully deal with the demands of life. (p. 41-42)

4. (a) Because women live mainly domestic lives they do not experience as many life transitions. (b) Care-giving roles help women develop strong bonds that lead others to care for them in old age. (c) Women's lives are full of transitions; thus, they learn to cope well with change. (d) Older women often gain status as they age. (p. 43-44)

5. Uhlenberg thought that influence was related to (a) the amount that your decisions influence others, (b) the ability to control how money is spent, and (c) the amount of status your current role has. (p. 46)

Chapter 2: DIVERSITY

6. Babysitting as a prelude to parenting; cohabitation as a prelude to marriage; childbirth classes as a prelude to actual birth; participation in preretirement classes as a prelude to retirement. (p. 50-51)

7. Schermerhorn said that an ethnic group was a collection of people within a larger society who had a common ancestry, memories of a shared history, and religious, linguistic, physical, or kinship pattern similarities. Helzberg stated that ethnicity was defined by a broader cultural criteria including a common language or customs. (p. 52-53)

8. Double jeopardy refers to simultaneously belonging to an ethnic minority (originally used only for African Americans) and being old. Most researchers have abandoned the concept because it tends to ignore many key factors that actually may be at the base of social inequities. (p. 53-54)

9. Bastida reported several interesting trends including: (a) All age groups used realistic age group qualifiers to describe themselves. (b) Strong age norms were reported for grooming, courtship, marriage and ability to discuss sexuality. (c) Women were much harsher in enforcing the norms. (d) Few differences were found for Mexican, Puerto Rican, and Cuban subgroups. (p. 56-57)

10. Luborsky and Rubinstein concluded that (a) the meaning of ethnic identity is based on past personal and family experiences; (b) ethnic identity is derived from specific historical events; (c) ethnic identity can be evoked in specific settings and under circumstances of specific need; (d) ethnic identity is dynamic and is continually rethought; and (e) ethnic identity gains importance as we age. (p. 57-58)

11. There are numerous cultural differences in status determination. Cross-culturally, some of these include (a) the lack of specific terms to discuss periods of life (e.g., no "middle age" or "old man"); (b) in some African cultures personhood is obtained only with the production of grandchildren; (c) many cultures view death as a stage of life; and (d) many cultures make a distinction on women on the basis of their reproductive status. (p. 60-61)

12. The U.S. fits best into the ranked horticultural society. We have a large population and a hierarchical political system (with a president and Congress). We also follow the general trend of devaluation of the elderly found in most industrialized societies. (p. 63-65)

13. While it may have been a historically accurate statement, a look at modern Asian societies (e.g., Japan) leads us to a different conclusion. For example, several studies have shown a growing reluctance among middle age children to care for their elderly parents. (p. 66-68)

Chapter 2: DIVERSITY

IV. AFTER THE FACTS

1. What impact will a significantly older population have on our country's social and economic priorities? How will your life be affected by these changes?

2. It has been suggested that older Americans will not make many gains in status or importance. Do you agree with this assessment? If not, why do you think things will be different?

3. Given the anticipated increase in the number of elderly minority persons and current racial problems, what problems do you see arising in the next 20 years? How would you address these problems?

4. As you have read, different cultures have different attitudes toward aging and the elderly. Which systems do you prefer? How well does our current U.S. system match your preferred system?

V. REVIEW ANSWERS

Terms to Know
Check the Key Terms section for Chapter 2 (p. 70)

True/False Answers
1. False (p.36)   6. False (p.49)
2. True (p.37)   7. True (p.57)
3. False (p.40)   8. False (p.61)
4. True (p.43)   9. True (p.63)
5. True (p.43)   10. False (p.66)

Fill-in-the-Blank(s) Answers
1. increase significantly (p. 41)
2. cohort flow (p. 45)
3. societal significance (p. 45)
4. anticipatory socialization (p. 50)
5. resocialization (p. 51)
6. ethnogerontologist (p. 51)
7. double jeopardy (p. 53); African-American (p. 53)
8. acculturation (p. 58)
9. Modernization (p. 64)
10. age-based (p. 64)

Multiple Choice Answers
1. A (p.36)   9. D (p.45)   17. C (p.55)
2. C (p.37)   10. A (p.46)   18. B (p.56)
3. C (p.37)   11. B (p.47)   19. C (p.58-59)
4. D (p.39)   12. C (p.49)   20. D (p.61)
5. A (p.39)   13. D (p.51)   21. C (p.62)
6. A (p.41-42) 14. A (p.52)   22. A (p.63-64)
7. B (p.43)   15. B (p.53)   23. D (p.68)
8. B (p.44-45) 16. D (p.54)   24. D (p.70)

CHAPTER 3
PHYSIOLOGICAL CHANGES

I. PREVIEW

Focus Questions

☞ **Why does physical aging occur?**
(Focus on: Intrapersonal Factors and Attempts at Explaining Aging)

☞ **How does your brain change with age?**
(Focus on: Structural Changes in the Neuron)

☞ **How can we study changes in brain structure and function?**
(Focus on: Studying Brain-Behavior Relations: Imaging Techniques)

☞ **What are the distinguishing features of the major types of cardiovascular disease?**
(Focus on: Cardiovascular Disease)

☞ **Do vision, hearing, taste, smell, and touch decline in old age?** (Focus on: The Senses)

☞ **What are the key reproductive changes that occur during middle adulthood?**
(Focus on: Reproductive Changes in Women; Reproductive Changes in Men)

Chapter 3: PHYSIOLOGICAL CHANGES

Chapter Outline

II. REVIEW

Terms to Know

Write your own brief definition for each of the following terms.

Angina:

Atherosclerosis:

Cerebrovascular Disease:

Chronic Obstructive Lung Disease (COLD):

Cross-Linking:

Dendrites:

Emphysema:

Free Radicals:

Hayflick Limit:

Hypertension:

Ischemic Heart Disease:

Light Adaptation:

Lymphocytes:

Menopause:

Neuritic Plaques:

Neurofibrillary Tangles:

Neurotransmitters:

Osteoarthritis:

Osteoporosis:

Presbycusis:

Presbyopia:

Programmed Cell Death:

Rheumatoid Arthritis:

Vestibular System:

Wear-and-Tear Theory:

True/False Questions

____ 1. The wear-and-tear theory of aging offers the best explanation for global age-related changes.

____ 2. Chemical agents called neurotransmitters are released by one neuron and absorbed by the next neuron.

____ 3. Parkinson's disease appears to be caused by an excess of acetylcholine.

____ 4. The CT scan relies on the use of X-rays to ascertain brain structure.

____ 5. Women have significantly less incidences of cardiovascular disease.

____ 6. Arteriosclerosis is the most common type of heart disease found in older adults.

___ 7. Few visual changes occur after age 65.   *

___ 8. Hearing loss in the elderly appears to have little impact on communication patterns or interpersonal relationships.

___ 9. Menopause is often accompanied by the cessation of all sexual activity.

___ 10. Wrinkles are genetically programmed and for the most part not preventable.

Fill-in-the-Blank(s)   Questions

1. The fact that cell life appears limited to about 50 divisions is referred to as the _____.

2. _____ involves the interaction of different hormones and results in tissue stiffening.

3. The basic cell found in the brain is called a(n) _____.

4. When brain cells die, they may cluster around a core protein and form _____.

5. _____ are the part of the human immune system responsible for defending against viral infections and cancerous cells.

6. _____ is the cardiovascular problem caused by the buildup of fat within arteries.

7. The most serious type of _____ is _____, which involves an irreversible destruction of membranes around the air sacs in the lung.

8. _____ results from a buildup of pressure within the eye, whereas _____ are caused by the development of opaque plaques on the lens.

9. Balance is governed by the _____, and research has shown that the likelihood of falling _____ with age.

10. Changes in the reproductive system are generically referred to as _____. In women the most pronounced of these changes involves the cessation of menstruation, which is called _____.

Multiple Choice Questions

1. Some theorists argue that aging is caused by destruction caused by unstable _____, which damage cells.
   A. free radicals
   B. scavenger cells
   C. electro-isotopes
   D. t-molecules

2. A version of _____ theory focuses on the relationship between stress and aging.
   A. metabolic process
   B. cellular
   C. programmed cell death
   D. wear-and-tear

3. _____ theories of aging best account for the findings that Okinawans have a significantly greater lifespan than the average Japanese.
   A. Metabolic
   B. Cellular
   C. Programmed cell death
   D. Wear-and-tear

4. Kohn (1985) defined diseases as
   A. universal, progressive, and age related.
   B. age-related but not universal or inevitable.
   C. not age-related.
   D. all of the above

5. _____ are **not** typically observed in the human brain until very old-age.
   A. Neurofibrillary tangles
   B. The neurotransmitters dopamine and serotonin
   C. Neuritic plaques
   D. Neurons with multiple dendrites

6. Buell and Coleman's (1979) research demonstrated that
   A. only adult humans have neurotransmitters.
   B. dendritic growth may occur in the elderly.
   C. as we age our synapses grow farther apart.
   D. the cell body doubles in size between ages 20 and 60.

7. _____ is highly effective in assessing the metabolic processes of the brain.
   A. Computed tomography (CT scan)
   B. Positron emission tomography (PET scan)
   C. Magnetic resonance imaging (MRI)
   D. all of the above

8. Dementia occurs in about _____ of the elderly (those over age 65).
   A. 15%   C. 75%
   B. 50%   D. 95%

9. Sometimes immune system cells begin to form antibodies to attack healthy tissue. This process is called
   A. AIDS.   C. bacterial infarction.
   B. autoimmunity.   D. cellular cannibalism.

10. During a normal 75-year lifespan, the human heart pumps the equivalent of about _____ gallons of blood through the body.
   A. 900   C. 9,000,000
   B. 90,000   D. 900,000,000

11. Two common age-related changes in the heart involve
    A. the accumulation of fat deposits and stiffening caused by calcification.
    B. an increase in left ventricle size and a change in right ventricle shape.
    C. an increase in systolic blood pressure and a decrease in diastolic blood pressure.
    D. an increase in ventricular artery connections and a decrease in overall blood pressure.

12. People with _____ typically have no symptoms and are unaware of the existence of a problem.
    A. angina   C. hypertension
    B. a myocardial infarction   D. a cerebrovascular accident

13. _____ is the leading cause of blindness in the U.S.
    A. Accidental eye injury   C. Diabetic retinopathy
    B. Macular degeneration   D. Glaucoma

14. The inability to visually accommodate nearby objects results in
    A. dark adaptation problems.   C. presbyopia.
    B. light adaptation problems. D. sensitivity to glare.

15. Presbycusis involves a loss in the ability to hear
    A. spoken language.   C. in one ear.
    B. high-frequency sounds.   D. human speech.

16. The most significant single factor in hearing loss is
    A. aging.   C. stress.
    B. noise.   D. heredity.

17. Research on the elderly has indicated that the sense of _____ does not appear to change much with age.
    A. smell
    B. balance
    C. taste
    D. touch

18. A study of olfaction conducted by the National Geographic Society indicated that older persons had trouble detecting the smell of
    A. the substance added to natural gas to provide its odor.
    B. smoke.
    C. almost all food products.
    D. all of the above

19. Older males typically experience
    A. a significant decline in sperm count.
    B. less time needed to achieve an erection.
    C. a significantly shorter resolution phase between orgasms.
    D. no symptoms of reproductive change.

20. _____ is a factor in the formation of a wrinkle.
    A. The thinning of the outer skin layer
    B. The destruction of collagen fibers
    C. The loss of supporting layers of fat
    D. all of the above

21. Which statement concerning aging and hair is **true**?
    A. Men lose facial and head hair at the same rate.
    B. Women do not experience hair loss.
    C. Thinning of the hair is inevitable with age.
    D. Loss of hair can now be stopped for most people.

22. Research on muscle development has shown that
    A. the amount of body tissue declines with age.
    B. muscle strength does not diminish significantly during middle adulthood.
    C. the improvement rate with exercise does not vary with age.
    D. all of the above

23. Osteoporosis is a degenerative bone disease that results when
    A. more bone mass is lost than is produced.
    B. the bone that is produced is heavier than that which the supporting tissue can hold.
    C. calcium builds up in the remaining bone.
    D. high estrogen levels create faulty bone.

24. Rheumatoid arthritis
    A. is inherited.
    B. involves damage to bone material.
    C. may be treated by nonsteroidal anti-inflammatory drugs.
    D. all of the above

III. SHORT-ANSWER ESSAY (QUESTIONS AND ANSWERS)

Questions

1. Differentiate between the wear-and-tear and cellular (free-radical, DNA, and Hayflick limit) theories of biological aging.

2. What criteria did Kohn use to distinguish normal aging from disease? Using this criteria, what disease might really be better thought of as part of normal aging?

3. Differentiate between neurons, dendrites, terminal branches, synapses, and neurotransmitters.

4. What kinds of disorders have been linked to changes in neurotransmitters?

5. Compare and contrast CT, MRI, and PET brain imaging techniques.

6. What is the relationship between antibodies, lymphocytes, and autoimmunity?

7. What is the difference between ischemic heart disease, cardiac arrythmia, angina, and myocardial infarction?

8. What methods are commonly used to prevent or treat atherosclerosis?

9. What is chronic obstructive lung disease (COLD)? How and why has the incidence of this disease changed in the past 20 years?

10. How do glaucoma and cataracts differ?

11. Identify the four inner ear changes that may result in presbycusis.

12. Describe typical somesthetic and balance changes found with age.

13. What are the major symptoms of menopause?

Answers

1. The wear-and-tear theory views aging as the process of deterioration of parts (such as is seen in any machine) because of use. Cellular theories all correlate aging with cell destruction. One cellular theory is the free radical theory, which is the belief that aging results from free radical molecules' destruction of the cell membrane, which ultimately leads to organ breakdown. DNA-based approaches hypothesize that aging results from replication mistakes or faulty DNA repair systems. The Hayflick limit equates aging with 50-limit cell division. (p. 77-78)

2. Normal aging was said to be universal, progressive, and irreversible. Atherosclerosis (involves fat deposits inside of arteries) would meet these criteria. (p. 78-79)

3. A neuron is a nerve cell found in the brain. A dendrite is a section of the neuron that resembles a branch of a tree. The function of a dendrite is to seek out and collect incoming electrochemical signals from other neurons. The terminal branches lie at the opposite end of the neuron from the dendrites. The purpose of the terminal branches is to release electrochemical information to be picked up by another neuron. The synapse is the gap across which energy is transmitted from the terminal branches of one neuron to the dendrite of another neuron. Neurotransmitters are special chemicals released by neurons that play a significant role in both thought and behavior. (p. 80-81)

4. Dopamine level reductions are linked to Parkinson's disease. Acetylcholine variations have been linked to memory loss, Alzheimer's and Huntington's diseases. Serotonin may be related to sleep disorders. (p. 83)

5. A CT (computed tomography) uses a series of X-rays to create a three-dimensional image of brain tissue. MRI (magnetic resonance imaging) uses magnetic fields and molecular alignment of brain material to create an image of brain tissue. A PET (positron emission tomography) utilizes radioactive isotopes, which are injected into the brain system, to chart where processing is taking place in the brain. (p. 83-84)

6. Our immune system is designed to defend the body against foreign invaders. Lymphocytes are specialized cells that provide defense against malignant cells (cancer), many infections, and some bacteria. They accomplish this by the production of antibodies that attack and destroy the invaders. Sometimes our immune system makes a mistake and begins to attack its own healthy tissue. This process is referred to as autoimmunity. (p. 85-86)

7. Ischemic heart disease is common in older adults and involves an insufficient supply of blood to muscle tissue. Cardiac arrythmias are irregular heartbeats that are common in older adults. The cause is unknown but appears to be related to levels of salts and minerals in the blood stream. Angina involves the restriction of a supply of oxygen to the heart resulting in chest pains and/or a burning sensation. This can be brought on during physical exertion. A myocardial infarction is better known as a heart attack. This occurs when the blood supply to the heart drops below the level needed to sustain heart muscle. If prolonged, the result is the death of heart muscle. (p. 89-90)

8. Common methods of prevention include reducing fat and cholesterol intake, quitting smoking, and increasing exercise. Treatments may include a coronary bypass (using a blood vessel from another part of the body to serve as a new coronary artery), angioplasty (using a catheter with a ballon-like device attached to clear blockages), or a laser to clear deposits. (p. 90)

9. Chronic obstructive lung disease (COLD), the most common and incapacitating respiratory disorder affecting older adults, results from the blockage of air passages in the bronchial tubes. COLD appears to be due to smoking, infection, inheritance, and pollution factors. Since the incidence of several of these potential causes has increased in the past 20 years, it is not surprising that incidences of deaths due to COLD has tripled since the 1960s. (p. 92)

10. Cataracts and glaucoma are both common eye diseases related to structural changes within the eye that result in loss of transmissiveness (involving the amount of light passing through the eye) and/or accommodation (the ability to focus). Glaucoma occurs when pressure builds up within the eye because of faulty drainage. The key to curing glaucoma is to reduce this pressure. Cataracts result when opaque spots build up on the lens and cause significant transmissiveness problems. This problem is typically correctable by surgically removing the tissue. (p. 94)

11. Presbycusis has been linked to (a) atrophy of sensory and receptor cells, (b) a stiffening of the vibrating structures in the inner ear (c) a diminished supply of nutrients to the inner ear, and (d) the loss of neurons in the pathway to the brain. (p. 98)

12. Touch sensitivity threshold on smooth skin increases with age. Temperature sensitivity does not appear to vary greatly with age. Data on pain sensitivity is mixed: Some studies show an increase and others a decrease with age. No changes have been seen in the kinesthetic sense. Changes in balance, however, have been found to vary with age. Specifically, we see increases in dizziness, vertigo, and the likelihood of falling. (p. 100-101)

13. Menopause refers to the cessation of menstruation. Symptoms can include hot flashes, chills, headaches, depression, nervousness, and other aches and pain. Although not all women report symptoms, most report some physical or psychological impact. (p. 102)

IV. AFTER THE FACTS

1. Given your newly acquired knowledge of physical development and aging, how have your perceptions of "you as an older adult" changed?

2. In what ways may research on AIDS increase our knowledge of the overall aging process?

3. Cardiovascular disease is the major killer in industrial nations. Are you "at risk" for any of these diseases? If so, what steps might you take to reduce your risk status?

4. How might our knowledge of sensory changes in the elderly allow us to build more effective housing, communication, and transportation devices for this population?

V. REVIEW ANSWERS

Terms to Know
Check the Key Terms section for Chapter 3 (p. 110-111)

True/False Answers
1. False (p.77)
2. True (p.80)
3. False (p.83)
4. True (p.84)
5. True (p.88)
6. False (p.89)
7. False (p.94-96)
8. False (p.98)
9. False (p.103)
10. False (p.104)

Fill-in-the-Blank(s) Answers
1. Hayflick limit (p. 77)
2. Cross-linking (p. 77)
3. neuron (p. 80)
4. neuritic plaques (p. 81)
5. Lymphocytes (p. 86)
6. Atherosclerosis (p. 90)
7. chronic obstructive lung disease (p. 92); emphysema (p. 92)
8. Glaucoma (p. 94); cataracts (p. 94)
9. vestibular system (p. 101); increases (p. 101)
10. climacteric (p. 102); menopause (p. 102)

Multiple Choice Answers
1. A (p.77)
2. A (p.77-78)
3. A (p.77-78)
4. D (p.78)
5. C (p.81)
6. B (p.82)
7. B (p.84)
8. A (p.85)
9. B (p.86)
10. D (p.87)
11. A (p.88)
12. C (p.91)
13. C (p.94)
14. C (p.95)
15. B (p.97)
16. B (p.98)
17. C (p.98-101)
18. A (p.99)
19. A (p.103)
20. D (p.104)
21. C (p.105)
22. D (p.106)
23. A (p.107)
24. C (p.107-108)

CHAPTER 4
HEALTH

I. PREVIEW

Focus Questions

☞ **What factors Influence your life expectancy?**
(Focus on: Genetic Factors in Longevity; Environmental Factors in Longevity)

☞ **How does stress influence health and aging?**
(Focus on: Stress and Health)

☞ **What physical problems are associated with smoking?**
(Focus on: The Hazards of Cigarette Smoking)

☞ **Is alcohol consumption helpful or harmful?**
(Focus on: Negative Effects of Alcohol; Benefits of Alcohol)

☞ **Can exercise make us live longer?**
(Focus on: Aerobic Exercise and Aging)

☞ **How do dietary needs change with age?**
(Focus on: Establishing Dietary Requirements)

☞ **How can we improve our overall health status?**
(Focus on: Health Promotion and Aging)

Chapter Outline

Special Sections
How Do We Know?
Something to Think About

II. REVIEW

Terms to Know
Write your own brief definition for each of the following terms.

Addiction:

Aerobic Exercise:

Average Longevity:

General Adaptation Syndrome:

Health Promotion:

High Density Lipoproteins (HDL):

Low Density Lipoproteins (LDL):

Maximum Longevity:

Stress and Coping Paradigm:

Type A Behavior Pattern:

Type B Behavior Pattern:

Wernicke-Korsakoff Syndrome:

True/False Questions

___ 1. When acute diseases are a major cause of death, there is a fairly linear relationship between age and death.
___ 2. Married people live an average of five years longer than unmarried people.

___ 3. People in executive positions are more prone to stress than laborers.

___ 4. Epinephrine (adrenaline) is often released during the exhaustion stage of the general adaptation syndrome.

___ 5. Type A personality people are much more likely to die following a heart attack than Type B people.

___ 6. If smoking were eliminated completely in our society, it would have only a minor effect on our country's overall health status.

___ 7. Alcohol consumption peaks between the ages of 30 and 45 and then shows a steady decline.

___ 8. Strenuous exercise done on a regular basis may actually increase mortality risk.

___ 9. Research on nutrition has demonstrated that changes in sensory abilities (e.g., vision, smell) may lead to nutritional problems.

___ 10. The incidence of cancer increases systematically with age.

Fill-in-the-Blank(s)   Questions

1. The current maximum longevity of a human is around _____ years.

2. _____ was the only major cause of death to increase in females in the 1980s.

3. Selye used the term _____ to describe the many environmental stimuli that causes a person to react.

4. The _____ paradigm views stress in terms of an interaction between a thinking person and the environment.

5. _____ personalities have been linked to an increased risk of cardiovascular disease.

6. _____ is a serious disorder related to long-term drinking that results in severe memory loss and disorientation.

7. Aerobic exercise takes place when you achieve _____.

8. Of the two types of cholesterol, _____ is often referred to as "bad" because it is involved with clogging of arteries, whereas _____ is often called "good" because it helps clear arteries of deposits.

9. Cancer is the _____ leading cause of death in the U.S.

10. _____, which emphasizes the importance of disease prevention, is a new approach to medical care. This approach is different from the traditional _____ model, which emphasizes treatment following discovery.

Multiple Choice Questions

1. _____ is an acute disease that was a significant cause of death in the U.S. in the early 1900s but has been virtually wiped out as a killer today.
   A. Measles   C. Syphilis
   B. Polio   D. all of the above

2. Which is **not** a characteristic of a chronic disorder?
   A. rapid onset   C. difficult to treat
   B. long duration   D. none of the above

3. Average longevity is defined as the age at which _____ of a cohort group born in a particular year will die.
   A. 25%   C. 75%
   B. 50%   D. 100%

4. Which of the following can have a major impact on life expectancy?
   A. Having long-lived parents
   B. Having a close relative with Alzheimer's disease
   C. Having a relative with cardiovascular disease
   D. all of the above

5. Kallmann's research on the impact of heredity on longevity demonstrated that most identical twins who had lived in different environments died
   A. within 1 year of one another.
   B. within 3 years of one another.
   C. about 10 years apart.
   D. about 30 years apart.

6. Which group in the U.S. has the highest average longevity?
   A. African-American males   C. white males
   B. African-American females   D. white females

7. During the _____ stage of the general adaptation syndrome, we may look normal but physiological damage such as hypertension or peptic ulcers may be developing.
   A. alarm   C. resistance
   B. reaction-formation   D. exhaustion

8. According to Lazarus and Folkman, a person who says "I don't have to worry about a plane crash because I never fly" is making a
   A. primary appraisal.   C. tertiary appraisal.
   B. secondary appraisal.   D. reappraisal.

9. Older people tend to report _____ issues as a major source of stress.
   A. financial   C. family
   B. social   D. work

10. When coping with problems, older persons have been found to seldom
   A. solve their problems.   C. seek information from others.
   B. have financial worries.   D. all of the above

11. Stress appears to lead to
    A. ulcers.
    B. headaches.
    C. cardiovascular disease.
    D. all of the above

12. Which is **not** part of the inoculation approach to stress management?
    A. conceptualization of the problem
    B. biofeedback to assess stress levels
    C. acquiring new coping skills
    D. application of coping skills

13. Smoking is estimated to be responsible for _____ of lung cancer cases.
    A. 25%
    B. 50%
    C. 75%
    D. 100%

14. Smokers who quit
    A. have about a 50 percent chance of relapse.
    B. typically do so on their own.
    C. drop their risk of lung cancer to about that of the normal population within five years.
    D. all of the above

15. Who has the lowest mortality rate?
    A. complete abstainers
    B. light drinkers
    C. moderate drinkers
    D. heavy drinkers

16. Which statement concerning alcohol use is **false**?
    A. Alcoholics Anonymous has a high success rate.
    B. More men are likely to be diagnosed as alcoholics.
    C. Given the same amount of alcohol, older people will have a higher blood-alcohol ratio than younger people.
    D. Most alcoholics begin drinking early in life.

17. Aerobic exercise is most beneficial to
    A. young adults.   C. old adults.
    B. middle-age adults.   D. all age groups

18. Research has shown that the elderly tend to exercise
    A. for physical health reasons.
    B. to be more attractive to younger people.
    C. as much as younger persons.
    D. all of the above

19. Research on age-related patterns of sleep has demonstrated that
    A. the total time per 24-hours spent sleeping does not change a
       great deal in adulthood.
    B. older people have an easier time initially falling asleep.
    C. younger people have a harder time falling asleep after they have
       been awakened.
    D. all of the above

20. Which of the following is detrimental to getting a good nights sleep?
    A. drinking alcohol   C. napping during the day
    B. eating or snacking in bed D. all of the above

21. Which of the following instructions would be unlikely to be found in
    a set of sleep-related stimulus-control instructions?
    A. "If you cannot fall asleep, get up and go to another room."
    B. "Lie down only when you intend to sleep."
    C. "If you cannot sleep, pick a spot on the bedroom ceiling to focus on
       until you relax."
    D. "Stay up as long as you wish if you are not tired."

22. It is unnecessary for older people to significantly increase their
    intake of
    A. proteins.   C. carbohydrates.
    B. vitamins.   D. all of the above

23. Which of the following is **not** a nutrition-benefit pair?
    A. high fiber to reduce colon cancer
    B. broccoli to reduce osteoporosis
    C. chocolate to reduce osteoarthritis
    D. low fat to reduce cardiovascular disease

24. Minkler and Pasick found that the elderly are often excluded from health promotion programs because
    A. they are not perceived as having any future.
    B. most adults don't suffer from acute disorders, which are the focus of such programs.
    C. by having already reached old age, they have demonstrated their knowledge of healthy life practices.
    D. all of the above

III. SHORT-ANSWER ESSAY (QUESTIONS AND ANSWERS)

Questions

1. Differentiate between acute and chronic diseases.

2. How do the concepts of average and maximum longevity differ? Also, what would the average and maximum longevity be for a twenty-year-old college student?

3. What is the Human Genome Project?

4. List some of the environmental factors that can influence longevity.

5. Why do women live longer than men?

6. What stages did Selye include in his theory of stress and adaptation?

7. What were Lazarus and Folkman's types of stress appraisal?

8. What factors have been associated with effective coping?

9. How do Type A and Type B people differ? What is the impact of this difference?

10. What are some of the hazards associated with smoking?

11. How do the effects of alcohol vary with age?

12. List some common causes of age-related sleep disturbances.

13. What is the relationship between cancer risk and age?

Answers

1. Chronic diseases increase in incidence with age, have a slow onset, are long in duration, and continue to play a major role in the deaths of the old and aging. Acute diseases decline in incidence with age, have a rapid onset, a brief duration, and are no longer a major killer of the elderly in the U.S. (p. 114)

2. Average longevity is also called average life expectancy. It is defined as the age at which half of the individuals born in a particular year will die. Keeping in mind that average longevity varies by age, race, and other factors, the typical U.S. twenty-year-old male has a life expectancy of about 68 years and a typical U.S. female has a life expectancy of about 75 years. Maximum longevity is a species specific estimate of the maximum amount of years any member of that species could live. Current estimates place the maximum human longevity at around 120 years. (p. 116-117)

3. The Human Genome Project is designed to map out the entire human gene pattern. This information would then be used to cure diseases and increase longevity through gene splicing and replacement techniques. (p. 117-118)

4. Environmental factors include diseases, social class, exposure to environmental toxins (chemical and pollutants), diet, drinking, smoking, access to medical care, marital status, and sleep habits. (p. 118)

5. Part of the advantage appears to be genetic in that women are less susceptible to many diseases and genetic defects. The environment also plays a role, and researchers have pointed to work roles and smoking as being two areas that have historically given women a longevity advantage. (p. 119-120)

6. Selye's general adaptation syndrome hypothesized that when individuals encounter stress in the environment, they first act with alarm. In this alarm stage, a body's physiological defense mechanism (i.e., the sympathetic nervous system) is activated. The second stage is called resistance. In this stage, we attempt to cope with the stressor. In the final stage, exhaustion, the ability to resist the stressor is lost and the result may be psychological (e.g., depression) or physiological (e.g., cardiovascular) damage. (p. 120-122)

7. Lazarus and Folkman saw primary appraisals occurring when you decide whether an event may have a potential personal impact. Secondary appraisal concerns your perceived ability to cope with a stressor. Reappraisal occurs when we rethink our position when we become aware of a change in a stressor. (p. 122)

8. Coping appears to be dependent on many factors, including health, a positive attitude about your capabilities, effective problem-solving skills, good social skills, available social supports, and adequate financial resources. (p. 122-123)

9. Type A personalities tend to be competitive, angry, intense, and impatient. This style has been associated with high risk for cardiovascular disease. Type B personalities have a more relaxed style of dealing with life and stress. Research has revealed a lower risk of heart disease for Type Bs than for Type As, even when smoking, hypertension, and other risk factors are controlled. One interesting note is that despite being more susceptible for problems, if a heart attack does occur, Type As may actually recover better than Type Bs. (p. 124-126)

10. Smoking has been linked to an increase in emphysema, lung cancer, tongue cancer, bladder cancer, cancer of the larynx, angina, atherosclerosis, heart attacks, and low-birth weight in infants of mothers who smoke. In addition, secondhand smoke may also increase the risk of lung disease and cancer. (p. 127-128)

11. While alcohol affects the young and old in the same general way, some age-related differences have been observed. First, older people appear to have greater cognitive impairment following a single drink. Second, small amounts of alcohol in the elderly may prevent the body from clearing other drugs in the system. Finally, given the same amount of alcohol, older persons tend to have a higher blood-alcohol ratio. (p. 130-131)

12. Common causes of sleep disturbances include respiratory problems, physical illness and/or pain, medication, alcohol use, caffeine and nicotine use, stress, napping, and using the bed for purposes other than sleep. (p. 135-137)

13. The risk for all cancers increases as age increases, with a significant increase in the post-forty years. (p. 140-141)

IV. AFTER THE FACTS

1. Assume that in the next ten years scientists identify the specific causes of aging and are able to significantly lengthen the lifespan. What kinds of impact would this have on our society?

2. What methods do you typically use to cope with stress? Are these strategies contributing to the rate at which you are aging? If so, are there coping methods that might be better for you to try?

3. Both tobacco and alcohol have been linked to health problems. How could we realistically reduce the consumption rates of these products?

4. Based on the information covered in the chapter, what nutrition and life-style related changes might be most beneficial in helping you extend your life?

V. REVIEW ANSWERS

Terms to Know
Check the Key Terms section for Chapter 4 (p. 146-147)

True/False Answers
1. True (p.114)
2. True (p.118)
3. False (p.120)
4. False (p.121)
5. False (p.125)
6. False (p.127)
7. True (p.129)
8. True (p.133)
9. True (p.138)
10. True (p.140-141)

Fill-in-the-Blank(s) Answers
1. 120 (p. 116)
2. Smoking-related lung cancer (p. 120)
3. stressor (p. 120)
4. stress and coping (p. 122)
5. Type A (p. 124)
6. Wernicke-Korsakoff syndrome (p. 130)
7. a pulse rate of 60%-90% of your maximum heart rate (p. 132)
8. low density lipoproteins (p. 139); high density lipoproteins (p. 139)
9. second (p. 140)
10. Health promotion (p. 142); biomedical (p. 142)

Multiple Choice Answers
1. D (p.114)
2. A (p.114)
3. B (p.116)
4. D (p.117)
5. B (p.117)
6. D (p.118-119)
7. C (p.121)
8. A (p.122)
9. B (p.123)
10. C (p.123)
11. D (p.123-124)
12. B (p.127)
13. C (p.127)
14. B (p.128-129)
15. B (p.131)
16. A (p.129-131)
17. D (p.132-133)
18. A (p.133)
19. A (p.134)
20. D (p.136)
21. C (p.137)
22. D (p.139)
23. C (p.139-140)
24. A (p.143)

CHAPTER 5
INFORMATION PROCESSING

I. PREVIEW

Focus Questions

☞ **Do older adults attend to information in the same way as young adults?**
(Focus on: Selectivity; Capacity)

☞ **What factors are involved in keeping someone focused on a task?**
(Focus on: Vigilance)

☞ **Do reaction times slow as we age?**
(Focus on: Age Differences in Components of Reaction Time)

☞ **What factors lead to age-related slowing of responses?**
(Focus on: What Causes Age-Related Slowing?)

☞ **How safe are older drivers?**
(Focus on: Driving and Highway Safety)

☞ **What factors lead to language comprehension difficulties in later life?**
(Focus on: Language Comprehension and Sensory Systems; Language Comprehension and Information Processing)

Chapter 5: INFORMATION PROCESSING

Chapter Outline

Chapter 5: INFORMATION PROCESSING

II. REVIEW

Terms to Know
Write your own brief definition for each of the following terms.

Capacity:

Divided Attention:

Feature Integration Theory (FIT):

Human Factors:

Implicit Memory:

Information-Processing Approach:

Reaction Time:

Response Complexity:

Response Preparation:

Selectivity:

Sensory Memory:

Spatial Cuing:

Vigilance:

Chapter 5: INFORMATION PROCESSING

True/False Questions

____ 1. The information-processing approach assumes that humans are passive reactants to environmental stimuli.

____ 2. Researchers agree that all sensory information is passed directly into the working memory system.

____ 3. Research has shown that only younger adults become automatic on vigilance tasks.

____ 4. Flying a plane is a good example of a simple reaction-time task.

____ 5. Most researchers agree that age-related slowing occurs because of changes in higher-level cognitive processes rather than changes in the body.

____ 6. Information generated by human factors psychologists has seldom been used in the design of consumer products.

____ 7. Older adults have a much harder time identifying the messages on icon-based highway signs.

____ 8. It is critical to remember that age alone does not cause accidents.

____ 9. When words are presented in normal sentences at a rate of 400 per minute, older people are about 90-percent accurate at word identification.

____ 10. Research has indicated that interrupted speech is the hardest type for the elderly to comprehend.

Fill-in-the-Blank(s)   Questions

1. Every memory that a person has begins as a _____.
2. Showing a picture to a subject for a brief time and then displaying another picture directly over the spot where the first was displayed is one way to measure _____ using the _____ technique.

3. Differences in visual search abilities between young and old subjects can be eliminated by providing older subjects with _____.

4. Research has supported the hypothesis that _____ are greatly affected when older adults receive ambiguous information about a task. Such data supports the idea that age-related response declines occur because of problems in response _____.

5. Salthouse's work on the applied task of typing showed _____ concerning age-related slowing.

6. _____ psychology focuses on the interaction between humans and the physical environment.

7. Being able to remember the name of an obscure TV actor is an example of language _____.

8. The normal age-related loss of high-end sound frequencies is referred to as _____.

9. _____ words contain two syllables and have equal accent placed on each syllable (e.g., softball).

10. An _____ task assesses memory processes without deliberately having people learn specific material.

Multiple Choice Questions

1. Which is a fundamental question raised by the information-processing approach?
   A. Are there age differences in working memory?
   B. Are changes due to input (encoding) factors?
   C. Are changes due to output (retrieval) failures?
   D. all of the above

2. _____ is **not** of great interest to information-processing theorists.
   A. Sensory memory   C. Reinforcement
   B. Attention   D. none of the above

3. Feature integration theory (FIT) focuses on
   A. feature extraction and feature integration.
   B. encoding and storage.
   C. short-term and long-term memory.
   D. attention and retention.

4. The selective attention skills of older people are greatly improved
   if they are provided with
   A. spatial cues as to where the item will appear.
   B. an attention-switching type task.
   C. better glasses.
   D. all of the above

5. Problems in selective attention in an older subject would be most
   pronounced if
   A. the relevant information were presented auditorily and the
   irrelevant information were presented visually.
   B. the relevant information were presented to the left hemisphere
   and the irrelevant information were presented to the right
   hemisphere.
   C. both the relevant and irrelevant information were presented
   visually.
   D. both the relevant information and irrelevant information were
   presented to the right hemisphere.

6. Capacity allocation on tasks of vigilance show
   A. that younger people are superior to older people.
   B. that older people are superior to younger people.
   C. no age-related differences.

7. _____ has been so well documented that it represents one of
   the only "universal behavioral changes" that is accepted by almost
   all gerontologists.
   A. Losses in memory capacity   C. The development of dementia
   B. Slowing down with age   D. Arthritis

8. On _____ reaction-time tasks, older people perform slower than younger people.
   A. simple   C. complex
   B. choice   D. all of the above

9. When the level of uncertainty concerning a task is equalized,
   A. younger subjects outperform middle-age and older adults.
   B. older adults outperform young and middle-age adults.
   C. middle-age adults outperform younger and older adults.
   D. no age-related differences can be found.

10. The neural network model predicts that information processing may be influenced by all of the following **except**
    A. the number of neural links for a given process.
    B. the length of a neuron.
    C. the death of a neuron.
    D. the production of neural bypasses.

11. The Myerson model of information loss hypothesizes that the biggest contributor to age-related information loss involves
    A. the lack of experience found in most older adults.
    B. the accelerated rate at which information is lost in the elderly.
    C. the wide gap between the number of elderly females versus elderly males.
    D. all of the above

12. Older race car drivers appear to avoid accidents by
    A. not getting into situations that require a quick response.
    B. maintaining reflexes as quick as younger drivers.
    C. driving slower.
    D. relying more on mechanics than on their driving skills to increase car speed.

13. Practice _____ age-related differences found on reaction time tasks.
    A. does not effect
    B. has a minimal effect on
    C. considerably lessens
    D. eliminates

14. Physical exercise
    A. has no effect on reaction times.
    B. may have a minimal effect on reaction times.
    C. has been shown in several studies to greatly improve reaction times.

15. Which product would likely have been "invented" by a human factors psychologist?
    A. automobile air-bags
    B. automatic shut-off switches on irons
    C. the layout of an automatic teller machine (ATM)
    D. all of the above

16. Older adults
    A. have significantly more accidents than younger adults.
    B. are more likely to drive in bad weather.
    C. have more trouble filtering out irrelevant road information.
    D. all of the above

17. Older adults' driving problems seem to be related to all of the following **except**
    A. sensory deficiencies.
    B. perceptual deficiencies.
    C. reaction-time deficiencies.
    D. memory deficiencies.

18. Most at-home injuries involve
    A. electric shock.
    B. burns.
    C. falls.
    D. lacerations.

19. The most common cause of accidental death in persons between the
    ages of 65 and 74 involves a
    A. drug overdose.   C. fall.
    B. burn.   D. car accident.

20. Although older people constitute about 11 percent of the population,
    they account for about _____ of all accidental deaths.
    A. 9%   C. 41%
    B. 23%   D. 75%

21. _____ has been suggested as a way to lower the incidence of
    accidental injury in the elderly.
    A. Placing throw rugs over wood floors
    B. Having bus fares in hand before boarding the bus
    C. Raising the thermostat on the hot water heater
    D. all of the above

22. The first English phoneme affected by presbycusis would be
    A. /s/.   C. /d/.
    B. /g/.   D. /m/.

23. _____ affect(s) language comprehension in the elderly.
    A. The speed of presentation   C. The presence of background noise
    B. Interruptions   D. all of the above

24. Which statement concerning language is **false**?
    A. Normal losses of basic linguistic processes are responsible for
       most age-related changes in memory.
    B. Knowledge base can affect encoding richness.
    C. The context in which words are presented can affect one's ability
       to comprehend words.
    D. Language comprehension can be affected by sensory loss.

III. SHORT-ANSWER ESSAY (QUESTIONS AND ANSWERS)

Questions

1. What are the basic assumptions of the information-processing approach to development?

2. Identify methods for studying sensory memory.

3. Differentiate between attention selectivity, capacity, and vigilance.

4. Describe a visual search task. Then discuss how visual search abilities change with age.

5. Summarize the findings concerning divided attention and age-related change.

6. Identify the potential processes involved in vigilance. Then report on which of these has been found to change with age.

7. What factors appear to be related to the increased response preparation time needed by older people?

8. What is a neural network and how may it be related to age changes in thoughts and actions?

9. What are the basic assumptions of the the Myerson model of information loss?

10. What kinds of age-related changes have been associated with driving and accidents?

11. What factors influence language comprehension in older adults?

Answers

1. Theorists who have adopted an information-processing approach to development have made the following assumptions: (a) People are active participants in the process of information acquisition. (b) Change is both qualitative and quantitative. (c) Information is processed through a series of processes, stages, or storage systems. (p. 150)

2. Sensory memory is typically studied using one of three methods. Some researchers investigate how rapidly information enters the system (encoding speed). Other researchers are interested in the amount of information that the sensory store can handle (perceptual span). The third method (backward masking) measures the duration of the memory trace. In this technique, a subject is first briefly shown a target stimuli. This stimuli is then rapidly replaced with a second stimuli. The subject's task is to identify the original stimuli. (p. 151)

3. Selectivity concerns our ability to deal with a limited portion of sensory information in our environment. Capacity involves the amount of information we can process at any one time. Vigilance concerns our ability to maintain   task performance over an extended period of time. (p. 152-153)

4. Subjects in a visual search task are shown a set of stimuli that contain both target and nontarget items. The goal of the task is to determine the amount of disruption to processing speed and efficiency caused by the nontargets. Results have indicated that older people have difficulty with visual search tasks because they are slower at feature integration (i.e., putting pieces of information together). (p. 153-154)

5. Divided attention research has led us to the following hypotheses: (a) The more complex the task the greater the possibility of age-related decrements in processing. (b) There are no real age differences in the ability to perform multiple tasks simultaneously. (c) The level of feature integration may be a critical factor in determining the ease at which adults can solve a divided attention task. (p. 156-157)

6. Parasuraman pointed out that vigilance appears to be related to four processes: (a) alertness; (b) adaptation and expectancy; (c) sustained allocation of attentional resources; (d) automaticity. Subsequent research has supported the existence of age-related differences in the area of alertness (with older adults showing lower levels of arousal and vigilance) and automaticity (with a slight age-related decrease). (p. 157-158)

7. Studies of response preparation time have shown that several factors may be related to the processing slowdown seen in older people. Two critical factors are ambiguous advance information and/or a long delay between advance and actual task. (p. 160)

8. A neural network is a hypothetical model designed to conceptualize the relationship between information processing and brain physiology. The basic premise is that thought and action are produced through the activity of a series of neurons. One reason to expect age-related changes involves the high possibility of neural damage or death. Such a circumstance would necessitate the building of a new and longer pathway. The result would be slower processing. (p. 162-163)

9. The four critical assumptions made by the Myerson model of information loss are as follows: (a) Processing speed is determined by totaling the time needed during each stage of processing. (b) The length of each step depends on information available at the beginning of a task. (c) Each time we reprocess information some is lost. (d) The key age-related loss involves the rate at which information is lost. (p. 163)

10. Driving difficulty in old age has been associated with (a) changes in light and dark adaptation abilities leading to trouble driving at night or in bright sunlight; (b) psychomotor slowing increasing reaction times; (c) visual changes increasing the likelihood of having trouble reading signs; and (d) attentional declines leading to trouble when multiple information is needed to be processed. (p. 167-168)

11. A combination of information processing and physiological factors appear to be critical in the loss of language comprehension found in older adults. Some of these factors include (a) presbycusis, which results in the loss of high frequence sounds; (b) less rich encoding of information (e.g., do not take advantage of contextual cues); and (c) attentional losses, which make it harder to follow more than one conversation or to process rapidly presented speech. (p. 171-173)

IV. AFTER THE FACTS

1. Human factors psychologists are constantly inventing better human and machine interface systems. What kinds of new devices to assist the aging do you think might be generated in the next 25 years? Is there any device that you see yourself needing later in your life?

2. Given your new understanding of adulthood information-processing skills, do you think that we should place old-age limits on driving privileges? If so, what criteria might you use to screen drivers?

3. If you were teaching a group of older adults, what changes might you make to ensure that your class information was presented in the most efficient manner?

4. Now that you are aware of the high potential for in-home accidents among the elderly and some potential causes, what suggestions might you give to an architect designing a home for an elderly couple?

V. REVIEW ANSWERS

Terms to Know
Check the Key Terms section for Chapter 5 (p. 177)

True/False Answers
1. False (p.150)   6. False (p.166-167)
2. False (p.152)   7. False (p.167)
3. True (p.158)   8. True (p.169)
4. False (p.159)   9. True (p.172)
5. False (p.162)   10. True (p.173)

Fill-in-the-Blank(s) Answers
1. sensory stimulus (p. 151)
2. sensory memory (p. 151); backward masking (p. 151)
3. spatial cues (p. 154)
4. reaction times (p. 160); preparation (p. 160)
5. mixed results (p. 165)
6. Human Factors (p. 166)
7. production (p. 170)
8. presbycusis (p. 172)
9. Spondaic (p. 172)
10. implicit memory (p. 174)

Multiple Choice Answers
1. D (p.150)   9. A (p.160-161)   17. D (p.168)
2. C (p.151-153)   10. B (p.162-163)   18. C (p.168)
3. A (p.153)   11. B (p.163)   19. D (p.171)
4. A (p.154-155)   12. A (p.164-165)   20. B (p.171)
5. C (p.154)   13. C (p.164)   21. B (p.171)
6. C (p.158)   14. C (p.166)   22. A (p.172)
7. B (p.159)   15. D (p.166-167)   23. D (p.172)
8. D (p.158)   16. C (p.167-168)   24. A (p.171-174)

CHAPTER 6
MEMORY

I. PREVIEW

Focus Questions

☞ **What kinds of memory do psychologists study?**
(Focus on: Working Memory; Secondary Memory; Tertiary Memory)

☞ **How do retrieval abilities change as we age?**
(Focus on: Age Differences in Retrieval)

☞ **What factors make it easier for some people to recall the plot of a novel or a newspaper article?**
(Focus on: Person Variables)

☞ **What role do spatial abilities play in memory?**
(Focus on: Spatial Memory)

☞ **How are metamemory and on-line awareness different?**
(Focus on: Types of Memory Awareness)

☞ **What methods are used to assess abnormal memory functioning?**
(Focus on: Clinical Issues and Memory Testing)

☞ **Can we teach people to use memory more effectively?**
(Focus on: Training Memory Skills)

Chapter Outline

Special Sections
Something to Think About
How Do We Know?

II. REVIEW

Terms to Know
Write your own brief definition for each of the following terms.

Behavior Rating Scale:

Configurational Learning:

Metamemory:

On-Line Awareness

Prospective Memory:

Recall:

Recognition:

Rehearsal:

Secondary Memory:

Spatial Memory:

Tertiary Memory:

Working Memory:

Chapter 6: MEMORY

True/False Questions

____ 1. Many researchers point to changes in working memory as the source of language processing difficulties often encountered in later life.

____ 2. A multiple choice exam is an example of a recall task.

____ 3. A memory task that uses words such as "byte" or "video" may be biased against older people.

____ 4. There do not appear to be any age-related decrements in storage ability.

____ 5. An algorithmic retrieval strategy produces error-free performance.

____ 6. Younger adults have a clear advantage over older adults in remembering details of a text passage.

____ 7. Speed of presentation of discourse material has little impact on memory of the material.

____ 8. Older subjects tend to underestimate their performance abilities when they are unaware of the task they will be asked to complete.

____ 9. There is a clear distinction between normal and abnormal memory performance.

____ 10. Adults who can fantasize easily may have an easier time learning effective internal memory strategies.

Fill-in-the-Blank(s) Questions

1. The most widely used model for studying memory is the _____.

2. The key to keeping information in working memory involves the use of _____.

3. _____ focuses on memory for personal life events.

4. The two-stage model of memory focuses on the processes of _____ and _____.

5. Researchers using a _____ memory task would provide organizational hints to improve memory performance.

6. Recalling details from a book, magazine, movie, or television program is said to collectively involve memory for _____.

7. Having difficulty finding your car in a mall parking lot because you came out a different door than you went in demonstrates the influence that _____ can play in memory. The specific ability to recognize a location when it is viewed from a different orientation is termed _____ learning.

8. Knowledge about how your memory works is called _____.

9. Being conscious of what you are doing with your memory at any given point is referred to as _____.

10. Camp has been able to teach severely afflicted Alzheimer's patients to remember _____ through the use of a _____ technique.

Multiple Choice Questions

1. _____ memory has the smallest capacity.
   A. Working   C. Tertiary
   B. Secondary   D. all have identical capacities

2. Evidence has shown that the capacity of working memory
   A. declines with age.
   B. remains constant over time.
   C. increases with age.
   D. none of the above

3. Recall and recognition are examples of
   A. working memory.   C. tertiary memory.
   B. secondary memory.   D. sensory memory.

4. Remembering to show up on time for your final exam demonstrates that you have an effective
   A. working memory.   C. tertiary memory.
   B. secondary memory.   D. sensory memory.

5. Because it often includes very old and personal data, _____ memory can be a difficult thing to measure.
   A. working   C. tertiary
   B. secondary   D. sensory

6. Bahrick, Bahrick, and Wittlinger's research on the ability to identify a former high school classmate discovered that
   A. face recognition was almost 90 percent after 15 years.
   B. less than 20 percent of people could recall the name of a classmate after 35 years.
   C. less than 5 percent of 70-year-olds could recognize a classmate's picture.
   D. all of the above

7. Coleman, Casey and Dwyer examined records from the Harvard Longitudinal Studies and found that
   A. memory for having had a childhood disease was highly accurate in older adulthood.
   B. memory for having been a smoker was highly accurate in older adulthood.
   C. memory accuracy for childhood events was significantly better at age 50 than at age 40.
   D. all of the above

8. Studies of Nazi prison camp survivors have provided _____ support for the idea of "flash-bulb" memories.
   A. little   C. strong
   B. moderate

9. Howe's two-stage model of memory proposes that information passes through a(n)
   A. unmemorized state.
   B. partially memorized state.
   C. memorized state.
   D. all of the above

10. Older persons typically
    A. group data with similar meaning into an organized whole.
    B. do not continue to use organizational schemes if they are not required to do so.
    C. make effective use of imagery and mnemonic strategies.
    D. all of the above

11. Few age-related differences are found between young and old subjects when a _____ memory task is used.
    A. recall
    B. cued recall
    C. recognition
    D. working

12. Difficulty in keeping irrelevant information out of current memory leads to age-related differences on tasks assessing
    A. recall memory.
    B. cued recall memory.
    C. recognition memory.
    D. working memory.

13. Differences in memory for discourse between younger and older adults can be minimized if
    A. there is unlimited study time.
    B. long text passages are used.
    C. the task involves the identification of general information versus specific details.
    D. all of the above

14. Adams, Labouvie-Vief, Hobart, and Dorosz found that when retelling a nonfable story, older adults tended to
    A. use a literal style.
    B. use an integrative style.
    C. use a text-based style.
    D. forget most of the passage.

15. Performance on word-list tasks is **least** influenced by
    A. pacing.   C. prior knowledge.
    B. age.   D. general verbal ability.

16. When trying to recall the location of a landmark, older subjects are less likely than younger subjects to use _____ to assist in recall.
    A. the architectural style of the building
    B. natural landscaping
    C. symbolic significance of the building
    D. spatial cues

17. Older adults are _____ to remember themselves as having performed an act they actually only observed.
    A. less likely   C. just as likely
    B. more likely

18. Schematic knowledge appears to influence older people's memory for pictorial items by leading these subjects to
    A. replace modern items with objects from their childhoods.
    B. fill in memory blanks with an object that makes sense.
    C. remember words in a picture better than the picture itself.
    D. have superior memory for faces.

19. Older adults tend to expect significant age-related declines in
    A. the ability to remember places.
    B. the use of memory strategies.
    C. memory capacity.
    D. all of the above

20. Which of the following does **not** affect memory?
    A. Alzheimer's disease
    B. Wernicke-Korsakoff's syndrome
    C. Marfan's syndrome
    D. depression

21. The influence of severe depression on memory appears to
    A. increase significantly with age.
    B. remain fairly stable with age.
    C. decrease significantly with age.

22. Weschler's Memory Scale Revised is an example of a
    A. neuropsychological assessment device.
    B. neurological assessment device.
    C. questionnaire.
    D. behavior rating scale.

23. Harris suggested that external memory cues are most effective if
    they are
    A. passive rather than active.
    B. situation specific.
    C. given close to the time action is required.
    D. all of the above

24. Memory training appears to be most effective when
    A. the adult involved is highly verbal.
    B. a combination of strategies is used.
    C. the program changes a subject's emotional state.
    D. all of the above

III. SHORT-ANSWER ESSAY (QUESTIONS AND ANSWERS)

Questions

1. Describe the Campbell and Charness study of practice, algorithms, and aging.

2. Identify the difference between secondary and tertiary memory.

3. Identify some methods of reducing age-related deficits on secondary memory tasks.

4. What were the basic findings of the Wagenaar and Groeneweg study of Nazi prison camp survivors.

5. Describe the basic age-related differences in storage.

6. Compare and contrast free recall, recognition, and cued recall tasks. Then indicate the kinds of developmental changes found for each.

7. Are age-related decrements in memory the result of storage or retrieval problems?

8. Identify and provide an example of the key variables that appear to affect learning and memory for prose.

9. Identify the difference between age-related trends in everyday memory and list-learning performance.

10. Briefly identify some metamemory and on-line awareness age-related differences.

11. What role do nutrition and medication play in memory changes seen in older adults?

12. Differentiate the following types of memory assessment devices: a) questionnaires; b) behavior rating scales; c) neuropsychological tests.

13. Identify and provide an example of the four major methods proposed by Harris for improving memory.

Answers

1. Campbell and Charness investigated the capacity of working memory by teaching young, middle-age, and older adults an algorithm for squaring a two-digit number. Practice was found to reduce calculation errors in all groups; however, significant age differences in working memory efficiency remained with older persons performing poorer. (p. 182)

2. Secondary memory refers to the ability to remember large amounts of information over a long period of time. The ability to perform day-to-day functions (e.g., driving, reading, going to class on time) is highly dependent on secondary memory. Tertiary memory involves the long-term storage of facts learned early. It differs from secondary memory because the focus is on the retention of people and events data versus activities. (p. 182-186)

3. Several useful techniques have been identified that appear to reduce age-related differences on secondary memory tasks. Helpful suggestions include using a recognition versus a recall task, presenting information in an organized manner, slowing the pace of presentation, using familiar material. (p. 183-184)

4. The Wagenaar and Groeneweg study of Nazi prison camp survivors showed that memory for things like date of arrival and ID number were highly accurate; however, many other details appeared to be forgotten over the years since the event. (p. 186)

5. Data has shown that age-related decrements in processing appear to be a result of (a) older people's difficulty in connecting new information with information already in storage; (b) older people's lack of automatic organization of incoming information; and (c) older people's lack of spontaneous utilization of effective memory strategies. (p. 187-188)

6. In a free recall task, subjects are presented with a list of information and are later asked to write or state as many items from the list as they can remember. In a recognition task, subjects are presented with a list and are later shown a second list that contains both new and old items (from the original task). The subject is asked to identify the "old" items. A cued recall task is similar to a free recall task; however, some organizational hints are provided before or during later memory assessment. Data from these different types of tasks results in different age-related patterns of responding. On free recall tasks, younger subjects perform significantly better than older subjects. On recognition tasks, no age-related differences are found. On cued recall tasks, the gap between younger and older performance is reduced but not eliminated. (p. 189)

7. Age-related differences in memory appear to be related to both retrieval and storage decrements in older adults. In addition, retrieval differences appear to be more substantial, and not all memory tasks result in age-related differences. (p. 190)

8. Most research on prose learning has focused on one of the following factors: (a) person variables (e.g., education level, general verbal abilities); (b) task variables (e.g., presentation speed); and (c) text variables (e.g., ease of readability, organizational pattern). (p. 191-194)

9. In general, researchers have found that performance on everyday tasks is more similar between younger and older subjects than performance on list-learning tasks, which consistently demonstrate the superior performance of young over old. (p. 198)

10. In the area of metamemory, older adults tend to differ from younger adults in several ways: (a) They are more likely to believe that memory capacity will deteriorate with age. (b) They perceive themselves as having little control over memory. (c) They appear to lack a basic understanding of how memory works. Concerning on-line awareness, older subjects tend to (a) overestimate their abilities when they are unaware of the task; (b) underestimate their abilities when told to think about strategies; and (c) accurately assess their abilities following a task. (p. 199-201)

11. Recently researchers have begun to focus on the role nutrition may play in the development of memory problems. Although there are no clear answers, the following substances have been linked to memory deficits: (a) thiamine deficiency; (b) niacin deficiency; (c) vitamin B_{12} deficiencies; (d) alcohol use; and (e) sedatives. (p. 203)

12. Questionnaires are typically designed to assess a person's awareness of their current memory abilities (e.g., awareness of capacities, use of strategies, frequency of forgetting). Behavior rating scales are instruments used by an observer to assess a person's memory abilities. These screening devices often include specific tasks for the subject to perform and the observer to score (e.g., recall a list of words). Neuropsychological tests are comprehensive batteries designed to assess numerous aspects of cognitive functioning (e.g., primary memory, secondary memory, attention, perceptual-motor speed). The most effective memory assessment combines all the forementioned methods. (p. 204-205)

13. Harris proposed that memory may be improved through the use of the following methods: (a) training internal memory strategies (e.g., method of loci, use of acronyms, mental retracing); (b) memory exercise (e.g., repetitive practice); (c) physical treatments (e.g., drugs); and (d) external memory aids (e.g., calenders, notebooks, diaries). (p. 206-210)

IV. AFTER THE FACTS

1. How accurate is your memory for past events? Write down a few of your earliest memories and then check their accuracy with an older person who also witnessed the events.

2. How might the information concerning memory for discourse assist you in remembering information presented in **this** text?

3. How accurate are your metamemory skills? During the next several weeks, make some specific predictions concerning your ability to recall a specific set of information. Use the results of your "experiment" to improve future memory performance.

4. What impact on society might there be if scientists are able to find a way to eliminate memory loss?

V. REVIEW ANSWERS

Terms to Know
Check the Key Terms section for Chapter 6 (p. 212-213)

True/False Answers

1. True (p.181)	6. True (p.190)
2. False (p.183)	7. False (p.193)
3. True (p.184)	8. False (p.200)
4. False (p.187)	9. False (p.202)
5. True (p.189)	10. True (p.207-208)

Fill-in-the-Blank(s) Answers

1. information processing approach (p. 181)
2. rehearsal (p. 181)
3. Tertiary or autobiographical memory (p. 184-185)
4. storage (p. 187); retrieval (p. 187)
5. cued recall (p. 189)
6. discourse (p. 190)
7. spatial memory cues (p. 195); configurational (p. 196)
8. metamemory (p. 199)
9. on-line awareness (p. 199)
10. names of staff members (p. 206); spaced retrieval (p. 206)

Multiple Choice Answers

1. A (p.181)	9. D (p.187)	17. B (p.197)
2. D (p.182)	10. B (p.187-188)	18. B (p.198)
3. B (p.182)	11. C (p.189)	19. C (p.199-200)
4. B (p.182)	12. D (p.189-190)	20. C (p.202-203)
5. C (p.184)	13. D (p.190)	21. B (p.204)
6. A (p.185)	14. B (p.192)	22. A (p.205)
7. D (p.185)	15. B (p.194)	23. C (p.209)
8. A (p.186)	16. D (p.195)	24. D (p.210)

CHAPTER 7
INTELLIGENCE

I. PREVIEW

Focus Questions

☞ **What are the general theoretical approaches taken to describe and explain intelligence?**
(Focus on: Research Approaches to Intelligence)

☞ **Are there any basic elements of intelligence?**
(Focus on: Primary Mental Abilities)

☞ **What personal and group factors might have an impact on intelligence?**
(Focus on: Moderators of Intellectual Change)

☞ **Can we increase intelligence in old age?**
(Focus on: Modifying Primary Abilities)

☞ **Can a Piagetian approach describe effectively adult thinking patterns?**
(Focus on: Piaget's Theory; Going Beyond Piaget: Postformal Thought)

☞ **How are wisdom and expertise related?**
(Focus on: Expertise; Wisdom)

Chapter 7: INTELLIGENCE

Chapter Outline

II. REVIEW

Terms to Know
Write your own brief definition for each of the following terms.

Accommodation:

Assimilation:

Cognitive-Process Approach:

Crystallized Intelligence:

Encapsulation:

Fluid Intelligence:

Neofunctionalist Approach:

Optimally Exercised Ability:

Postformal Thought:

Primary Abilities:

Psychometric Abilities:

Secondary Mental Abilities:

Unexercised Abilities:

True/False Questions

____ 1. According to work by Sternberg, motivation and reading are key indicators of intelligence throughout the lifespan.

____ 2. A psychometric theorist would promote the use of a standard IQ test as a way to measure intelligence.

____ 3. The lowest level of intelligence, according to hierarchical structure theorists, would be reflected by an answer to a specific item on an IQ test.

____ 4. The use of longitudinal research designs appears to increase the likelihood of finding a correlation between declining intelligence and age.

____ 5. Fluid intelligence does not appear to change dramatically with age.

____ 6. Differences in educational background have been shown to have little impact on intelligence.

____ 7. The dual-process model proposes that pragmatic intelligence is a critical factor in adulthood.

____ 8. Conservation skills first appear in the concrete operational stage of development.

____ 9. Research has shown that high school students tend to think at higher levels of reasoning when confronted with problems of great personal salience.

____ 10. Older persons appear to be able to compensate for loss of performance speed with expertise.

Fill-in-the-Blank(s) Questions

1. Sternberg and others have hypothesized that intelligence is made up of _____ clusters of related abilities.

2. _____ theorists are interested in individual differences and plasticity in intelligence.

3. The ability to add or subtract carries the primary mental abilities factor label of _____ , while the ability to remember a limerick or complete a sentence is labeled _____.

4. Crystallized and fluid intelligence are examples of _____ mental abilities.

5. The two general trends found on tests of fluid versus crystallized intelligence are an age-related increase in _____ and an age-related decline in _____.

6. Research by Avolio and Waldman on the impact of occupation demonstrated that a person's occupation had _____ impact on intellectual performance.

7. In the dual-process model, the phrase _____ is used to discuss the first cognitive process, which concerns developmental changes in basic information-processing and problem-solving abilities.

8. The fact that young children believe that all people and objects experience the world exactly as they do was termed _____ by Piaget.

9. Several researchers have proposed a fifth stage of Piagetian development that follows formal operations. They refer to this stage as involving _____.

10. The term _____ is used by researchers to describe the process of having the processes of thinking (e.g., attention, memory) become connected to the products of thinking.

Multiple Choice Questions

1. Which of the following is an example of social competence?
   A. a good vocabulary   C. admission of mistakes
   B. articulate speech   D. all of the above

2. Which of the following is **not** a behavior typically associated with problem-solving?
   A. reasoning logically
   B. seeing all aspects of a problem
   C. identifying connections between ideas
   D. none of the above

3. According to research by Sternberg, _____ was a key indicator of intelligence in 50-year-olds.
   A. open-mindedness
   B. a willingness to learn and establish a career
   C. social activity
   D. being up on current events

4. According to hierarchical structure models of intelligence, the highest level on the intelligence hierarchy involves
   A. general intelligence.   C. secondary mental abilities.
   B. primary mental abilities.   D. third-order abilities.

5. _____ was **not** one of Thurstone's original primary mental abilities.
   A. Word fluency   C. Associative memory
   B. Perceptual speed   D. Mental rotation speed

6. Ekstrom, French, and Hartman have compiled a list of about _____ primary abilities that appears to be supported by empirical research.
   A. 2   C. 50
   B. 25   D. 100

7. _____ is **not** one of the currently accepted primary mental abilities.
   A. Estimation   C. Figural flexibility
   B. Inductive reasoning   D. Sensory memory

8. Crystallized intelligence
   A. includes vocabulary skills.
   B. increases as we age.
   C. is acquired through experience.
   D. all of the above

9. The different developmental patterns found for fluid and crystallized intelligence help us to explain the
   A. simplicity of the concept of intelligence.
   B. differential performance of older persons on practical versus lab-based tasks.
   C. high correlation between IQ tests and fluid and crystallized intelligence found across the lifespan.
   D. superior performance of older persons on novel tasks.

10. Research on the impact of cohort effects has indicated that age-related differences in performance on intelligence tests are best explained as being caused by
    A. age differences.
    B. differences in testing materials.
    C. generational differences.
    D. all of the above

11. Researchers have identified a link between health status and intelligence for all of the following **except**
    A. cardiovascular disease.   C. slightly elevated blood pressure.
    B. hypertension.   D. Alzheimer's disease.

12. Langer's research on mindlessness suggests that
    A. older people are more at-risk for con artists.
    B. nursing home patients should be given a say in decisions that concern them.
    C. people who are cognitively active show the least age-related cognitive declines.
    D. all of the above

13. Research extending the original project ADEPT has indicated that
    A. some age-related declines in fluid intelligence may be reversible.
    B. there is tremendous generalization of training to other tasks.
    C. test anxiety does not play a role in the intellectual performance of older adults.
    D. all of the above

14. Which statement would **not** be made by a neofunctionalist?
    A. An average group curve of intelligence may not reflect individuals within the group.
    B. Intelligence appears to consist of several components.
    C. The individual components of intelligence are often unrelated to one another.
    D. There are multiple developmental patterns of intellectual development.

15. In Denney's model of unexercised and optimally exercised abilities, performance on traditional laboratory tasks is most similar to performance on
    A. practical problems.
    B. unexercised abilities.
    C. moderately exercised abilities.
    D. optimally exercised abilities.

16. Denney's research found that _____ were best at solving practical problems.
    A. children
    B. young adults
    C. middle-age adults
    D. elderly adults

17. Piaget's first stage of development is called the
    A. sensorimotor stage.
    B. concrete operational stage.
    C. preoperational stage.
    D. content stage.

18. Hypothetico-deductive reasoning
    A. involves resolving ambiguity and arriving at the one correct solution.
    B. can be applied to real or imaginary situations.
    C. may lead to feelings of uneasiness when the solution does not match our expectations.
    D. all of the above

19. Research on Piagetian stages has found all of the following **except**
    A. only about 75 percent of adolescents can solve a formal operations problem.
    B. less than 5 percent of those over age 65 can solve a formal operations problem.
    C. estimates are that only about 30 percent of adults reach full formal operational thought.
    D. almost 95 percent of adolescents can solve a formal operations task if they are given appropriate feedback and practice.

20. Perry's landmark research on postformal thought hypothesized that at the highest stage, thinking people
    A. can hold different positions to which they are equally committed.
    B. rely on an authority figure for direction.
    C. shift toward relativism in thought.
    D. are tightly bound by the rules of logic.

21. Kitchener and Kings proposed a theory on the development of reflective judgement. Their highest "view of knowledge" was that knowledge is
    A. absolute and concrete.
    B. constructed via the process of reasonable inquiry into generalizable conjectures about the material world.
    C. certain but not immediately available.
    D. subjective, because what is known is known via perceptual filters that may alter reality.

22. Schaie's model of cognitive development hypothesizes that executive abilities are most critical during
    A. young adulthood.   C. older adulthood.
    B. middle adulthood.

23. Expertise may be related to
    A. the use of a novel approach to a problem.
    B. lots of practice performing a task.
    C. an extensive knowledge about a task.
    D. all of the above

24. Research on the relationship between age and wisdom has shown
    A. a high positive correlation between age and wisdom.
    B. a high negative correlation between age and wisdom.
    C. no real relationship between age and wisdom.

III. SHORT-ANSWER ESSAY (QUESTIONS AND ANSWERS)

Questions

1. Identify the major clusters of intelligence agreed upon by both experts and laypersons (be sure to give an example of each type).

2. Describe the basic premises of the major research approaches to intelligence.

3. Briefly describe a "hierarchical structure of intelligence" model.

4. What were the two major findings of Schaie's study of primary mental abilities and aging?

5. Briefly describe the six major second-order mental abilities discussed in the text.

6. Describe Project ADEPT.

7. Identify and discuss the basic concepts underlying the neofunctionalist's approach to intelligence.

8. Briefly describe the components and developmental patterns of the main problem types proposed in Denney's model of unexercised and optimally exercised abilities.

9. Identify the difference among the Piagetian concepts of assimilation, accommodation, and hypothetico-deductive reasoning.

10. Describe Kramer's three styles of thinking.

11. Summarize Schaie's stage theory of adult cognition.

12. What is the basic premise and criteria of the Dittmann-Kohli and Baltes model of wisdom?

Answers

1. Sternberg and his colleagues found that both experts and laypersons grouped intelligence in the following clusters: (a) problem-solving (e.g., logical reasoning, accurate decision making); (b) verbal ability (high reading skills, large vocabulary); and (c) social competence (e.g., displaying an interest in others, being on time). (p. 217)

2. The three major research approaches to intelligence are (a) the psychometric approach, which concentrates on the use of standardized paper-pencil tests to define and measure intelligence; (b) the neofunctionalist approach, which emphasizes individual differences and plasticity of thinking; and (c) the cognitive-process approach, which is most interested in the information-processing components that underlie thinking. (p. 218)

3. Hierarchical structure models view intelligence as an organization of lesser components into a greater whole. They see the lowest level of intelligence as consisting of answers to individual items on a test of intelligence. The next level would include a grouping of such items. The third level, often referred to as one's primary mental abilities, would reflect performance across several different intelligence tests. The next level, secondary mental abilities, combines performance across primary mental abilities. Third-order abilities represent performance across secondary mental abilities. At the top of the hierarchy is general intelligence which reflects performance across the third-order abilities. (p. 219)

4. While Schaie's study generated numerous interesting findings, the two most critical were: (a) Declines in all primary abilities were found for subject over age 60; and (b) Use of a cross-sectional design led to a significantly more pessimistic outlook in cognitive functioning in later life. (p. 221)

5. The six major secondary-order mental abilities discussed in the text are as follows: (a) Crystallized intelligence (Gc) reflects knowledge and experience you acquire throughout your lifetime. (b) Fluid intelligence (Gf) refers to your basic information-processing skills. (c) Visual organization (Gv) includes visualization, spatial orientation, and speed of closure. (d) Auditory organization (Ga) focuses on auditory cognitive factors such as speech perception and temporal tracking. (e) Short-term acquisition and retrieval. (f) Long-term storage and retrieval. (p. 221-223)

6. Project ADEPT was a comprehensive training study designed to determine if the intellectual performance of older adults could be improved. Two intervention methods were used: First, subjects were provided with a great deal of task familiarity. Next, subjects were given training designed to improve the specific primary abilities necessary for task solution. Results showed a significant increase in task performance; however, there appeared to be little transfer or long-term maintenance. (p. 230)

7. The neofunctionalist approach to intelligence is based on the concepts of (a) plasticity, the belief in the modifiability of cognitive abilities within a given range; (b) multidirectionality, the belief that intelligence in made of numerous components; (c) multidirectionality, the belief that different abilities have different developmental patterns; and (d) individual variability, the belief that because all individuals develop in different ways we need to focus more on intraindividual change. (p. 231-232)

8. Denny divided problem-solving potential into several types. Traditional laboratory-based problems tap information-processing skills. Unexercised abilities involve performance on unfamiliar tasks. Practical performance focuses on everyday tasks. Optimally exercised abilities center on a task with which the individual has a great deal of experience. The basic developmental pattern for all types is low in childhood, a peak in early middle-age, and a slow decline thereafter. The difference between the patterns involves superior performance on exercised (used) versus unexercised and lab-based tasks (unused). (p. 233-234)

9. Piaget believed that thought was governed by the principle of adaptation (adjusting to the environment). He broke down the concept of adaptation into two basic processes: (a) assimilation, in which a person makes use of currently held information and fits new information into an existing schema (idea); (b) accommodation, in which a person is unable to assimilate information and creates a new idea (schema) to fit the existing data. Hypothetico-deductive reasoning was a specific form of problem solving found in formal operations that involves forming and testing a hypothesis until it is confirmed or rejected. (p. 235-236)

10. Kramer's styles included (a) absolutist thinking, believing that there is only one answer and it can be found through personal experience; (b) relativistic thinking, realizing there are many possible answers to a question and the correct answer may change with circumstances; and (c) dialectic thinking, realizing that there are many different possible solutions to every problem and being able to synthesize them into a coherent whole. (p. 240-242)

11. Schaie hypothesized that cognitive development takes place in three stages. In adolescence and young adulthood, the focus is on acquisition of information. Middle adulthood is characterized by a focus on both executive (work-related) and responsible (relationship-related) issues. Old age involves reintegration of intellectual abilities into a more simplistic form. (p. 243-244)

12. The basic premise of the Dittmann-Kohli and Baltes model is that wisdom is defined as expert knowledge based on everyday life. Their five criteria were (a) expertise in practical aspects of everyday life; (b) breadth of ability to define and solve a problem; (c) being aware that problems differ with age; (d) being aware that correctness is dependent on personal goals and priorities; and (e) recognition that life is uncertain and complicated. (p. 246)

IV. AFTER THE FACTS

1. Have you reached the postformal stage of thinking? If yes, what are some examples of thinking that you might use to support your assessment?

2. From where do your primary mental abilities come? If they are "learned," can you think of ways to improve your intelligence?

3. Denney has speculated on the importance of "optimally exercised abilities." Think about your career plans and speculate on the types of optimally exercised abilities you may possess in later life.

4. Think about older persons you see as being "intelligent." Would you say that their intelligence is more a result of wisdom or expertise?

V. REVIEW ANSWERS

Terms to Know
Check the Key Terms section for Chapter 7 (p. 250)

True/False Answers
1. True (p.218)	6. False (p.225-226)
2. True (p.218)	7. True (p.232)
3. True (p.219)	8. True (p.236)
4. False (p.221)	9. False (p.242)
5. False (p.224)	10. True (p.245)

Fill-in-the-Blank(s) Answers
1. three (p. 217)
2. Neofunctionalist (p. 218)
3. Number facility (p. 220); Meaningful memory (p. 220)
4. secondary (p. 221)
5. experience-based processes (p. 225); information-processing abilities (p. 225)
6. a significant (p. 227)
7. cognition as basic processes (p. 232)
8. egocentrism (p. 236)
9. postformal thought (p. 240)
10. encapsulation (p. 245-246)

Multiple Choice Answers
1. C (p.217)	9. B (p.224-225)	17. A (p.235-236)
2. D (p.217)	10. C (p.225)	18. D (p.236-237)
3. B (p.218)	11. C (p.228)	19. B (p.237-238)
4. A (p.219)	12. D (p.228)	20. A (p.240)
5. D (p.217)	13. A (p.230-231)	21. B (p.241)
6. B (p.219)	14. C (p.232)	22. B (p.244)
7. D (p.220)	15. B (p.233-234)	23. D (p.245)
8. D (p.222-224)	16. C (p.233)	24. C (p.247)

CHAPTER 8
PERSONALITY AND MORAL DEVELOPMENT

I. PREVIEW

Focus Questions

☞ **What categories of personality traits are studied by psychologists?**
(Focus on: Costa and McCrae's Model; Some Specific Traits)

☞ **Do personality traits change as we age?**
(Focus on: Costa and McCrae's Model; Some Specific Traits; Conclusions About Personality Traits)

☞ **Are there stages of personality development in adulthood?**
(Focus on: Erikson's Stages of Psychosocial Development; Loevinger's Theory)

☞ **Do most people suffer a "midlife crisis?"**
(Focus on: Theories Based on Life Transitions)

☞ **What role might cognitive abilities play in personality development?**
(Focus on: Thomae's Cognitive Theory of Personality; Whitbourne's Life Story Approach)

☞ **Does moral thinking change with development?**
(Focus on: Kohlberg's Theory; Critiques of Kohlberg's Theory)

Chapter 8: PERSONALITY AND MORAL DEVELOPMENT

Chapter Outline

Special Sections

II. REVIEW

Terms to Know
Write your own brief definition for each of the following terms.

Conventional Level:

Ego Development:

Epigenetic Principle:

Life-Span Construct:

Moral Reasoning:

Personal Control:

Possible Selves:

Postconventional Level:

Preconventional Level:

Self-Concept:

Trait:

True/False Questions

   ___ 1. Sigmund Freud believed that personality development continued across the lifespan.

   ___ 2. A person who is habitually late would score high on a scale measuring conscientiousness.

____ 3. Researchers have found an increasing belief in self-inferiority in older adults.

____ 4. Age appears to be the best predictor of life satisfaction.

____ 5. Being a good parent would indicate a successful resolution of the generativity versus stagnation crisis.

____ 6. According to Loevinger, most adults in American society operate at an individualist stage of ego development.

____ 7. There is great support for the kinds of adult life transitions identified in the works of Sheehy and Levinson.

____ 8. Cognitive theorists propose that the way you perceive your life progressing is more important than how it actually is progressing.

____ 9. Research has shown that most people fear their future "intellectual self" more than any other possible self.

____ 10. The best predictor of a person's level of moral reasoning is his or her current level of cognitive functioning.

Fill-in-the-Blank(s) Questions

1. The term _____ is used to describe a fairly stable aspect of a persons personality.

2. A person that you call the "life of the party" would score high on a personality scale measuring _____.

3. Numerous studies have documented a shift from active to _____ mastery in later life.

4. Carl Jung believed that the best way to conceptualize personality development was to focus on the development of one's _____.

5. The _____ principle hypothesizes that development is driven by problems that occur at particular times of life.

6. Loevinger's highest stage of ego development was called the _____ stage and involved the ability to _____.

7. Whitbourne's cognitive approach to personality emphasizes the process of the life-span construct which is composed of the constructs of _____ and _____.

8. _____ is the organized pattern of self-perception.

9. _____ refers to the degree to which you believe that the outcome of a task depends on your personal characteristics.

10. In Kohlberg's highest stage of moral reasoning a person's decisions are based on _____.

Multiple Choice Questions

1. The basic argument made by cognitive theorists concerning the stability of personality during adulthood is that
   A. there is no stability.
   B. there is great stability.
   C. people tend to remain the same unless they feel the need to change.
   D. change is driven by biological maturation.

2. Personality traits are assumed to be
   A. based on comparisons with others.
   B. distinctive.
   C. stable.
   D. all of the above

3. Which of the following is **not** a facet of neuroticism?
   A. anxiety--hostility
   B. self-consciousness--depression
   C. manipulator--unsympathetic
   D. impulsiveness--vulnerability

4. A person who enjoys trying new types of foods in restaurants would score high on
   A. agreeableness.   C. extraversion.
   B. openness to experience. D. all of the above

5. The basic conclusion from the Costa and McCrae study of personality traits was that
   A. no traits exist.
   B. traits exist, but they change rapidly from year to year.
   C. traits appear to be stable over many years.

6. Results from the Berkeley longitudinal studies indicated that the best predictor for life satisfaction in old age for men involved
   A. personality traits.   C. life style in young adulthood.
   B. employment status.   D. educational background.

7. Which statement concerning life satisfaction is **false**?
   A. There is a strong correlation between age and life satisfaction.
   B. Health status and death of a spouse may artificially inflate negative feelings found in old age.
   C. Neuroticism and happiness are both related to satisfaction.
   D. Income level and marital status appear to be related to life satisfaction.

8. According to current gender-role stereotypes found in the world today,
   A. men are thought to become more war-like in old age.
   B. old women are believed to become evil persons who use their powers malevolently.
   C. the need for strong gender roles is believed to increase with age.
   D. all of the above

9. The best conclusion concerning the stability of personality traits across the lifespan is that
   A. personality traits appear to be stable if you look at a specific individual's development.
   B. personality traits appear to be stable if you average data across many different individuals.
   C. personality traits appear to be stable if you compare different ethnic groups.
   D. there is no evidence for stability of personality.

10. Carl Jung stated that to be psychologically healthy, a person must possess
    A. mostly an introverted orientation.
    B. mostly an extroverted orientation.
    C. a balance of introverted and extroverted orientations.
    D. neither introverted nor extroverted orientations.

11. According to Erikson, the first psychosocial crisis encountered by humans involves
    A. trust versus mistrust.   C. autonomy versus doubt.
    B. initiative versus guilt.   D. industry versus inferiority.

12. The basic strength of love is formed during the
    A. identity versus role confusion crisis.
    B. intimacy versus isolation crisis.
    C. generativity versus stagnation crisis.
    D. integrity versus despair crisis.

13. Logan stated that Erikson's model is really a cyclical progression from
    A. trust to achievement to wholeness.
    B. youth to adulthood to death.
    C. introversion to extraversion to integrity.
    D. sensitivity to selfishness to oneness.

14. The beginning of self-evaluated standards and the realization that you control your own future characterizes Loevinger's _____ stage of ego development.
    A. conscientious   C. autonomous
    B. individualistic   D. integrated

15. Loevinger assesses ego development using the
    A. MMPI.   C. WAIS-R.
    B. Sentence Completion Test.   D. strange-situation paradigm.

16. Which statement concerning research on the "midlife crisis" is **true**?
    A. Women typically list events like marriage and childbirth as major life crises.
    B. Most men find their careers unsatisfying and stress producing.
    C. The idea of a universal "midlife crisis" is more the result of media presentations than empirical research.
    D. all of the above

17. Results from the Bonn Longitudinal Study of Aging indicate that
    A. few older adults see themselves as having aged successfully.
    B. there appear to be numerous patterns of successful aging.
    C. a single score on a personality measure tends to be an accurate predictor of adult personality.
    D. there is little stability in adult personality.

18. According to Whitbourne, an overreliance on identity assimilation will lead to
    A. an overwillingness to change to fit the environment.
    B. the development of defense mechanisms.
    C. a midlife crisis.
    D. a great resistance to change.

19. Mortimer, Finch, and Kumka's longitudinal study of self-concept found that
    A. self-image consists of four dimensions: well-being, activity, unconventionality, and interpersonal qualities.
    B. the structure of self-concept changed little over time.
    C. changes in self-perception were highly related to specific life events.
    D. all of the above

20. Research on possible selves has shown all of the following **except**
    A. changes in physical self were highly feared by young and middle-age women.
    B. older people tend to have more multiple possible selves.
    C. younger adults see themselves as improving with age.
    D. fear of a possible self can be a highly motivating factor in determining a person's behavior.

21. The belief in high personal control
    A. increases with age.   C. varies by domain.
    B. is higher in women.   D. all of the above

22. A person relying on laws as their basis for making moral decisions (e.g., you should not steal because it is illegal) is operating at the _____ stage of development.
    A. individualism, instrumental purpose, and exchange
    B. mutual interpersonal expectations, relationships, and interpersonal conformity
    C. social system and conscience
    D. social contracts or utility and individual rights

23. On the "Heinz dilemma," if a person said that Heinz should steal the drug, that person could be operating at the _____ level of development.
    A. preconventional
    C. postconventional
    B. conventional
    D. all of the above

24. Which statement concerning moral development is **true**?
    A. Kohlberg's dilemmas appear to be biased against younger subjects.
    B. Moral development appears to follow a stage-like progression.
    C. Older subjects operate at similar levels of reasoning on both applied and hypothetical problems.
    D. all of the above

III. SHORT-ANSWER ESSAY (QUESTIONS AND ANSWERS)

Questions

1. Identify and briefly describe the five dimensions of Costa and McCrae's model of personality.

2. Briefly summarize the findings from research on gender-role identity across adulthood.

3. Discuss Jung's views on the development of introversion-extroversion and feminine-masculine in adulthood.

4. Describe the 5th through 8th psychosocial stages of Erikson's model of personality development.

5. Discuss Van Geert's model of stage movement within a Eriksonian framework.

6. Identify and describe major components of Loevinger's six stages of adult ego development.

7. Briefly discuss Thomae's three postulates of personality development.

8. Differentiate among Whitbourne's concepts of the scenario, the life story, identity accommodation, and identity assimilation.

9. Differentiate among Kohlberg's three levels of moral reasoning.

10. What were Gilligan's basic complaints concerning Kohlberg's theory of moral reasoning?

Answers

1. The Costa and McCrae model of personality focuses on the dimensions of (a) neuroticism (e.g., anxiety, fear, anger); (b) extraversion (e.g., warmth, assertiveness, excitement seeking); (c) openness to experience (e.g., fantasy, willingness to try something new, aesthetic appreciation); (d) agreeableness-antagonism (e.g., skeptical, aggressive, manipulators); and (e) conscientiousness-undirectedness (e.g., energetic, ambitious, persevering). (p. 255-257)

2. The issue of gender-role change in older adulthood has generated conflicting results. Several studies have found that there is a tendency for older males and females to adopt similar roles (i.e., see themselves as more nurturing and intimate). It appears, however, that this change in personal belief often does not result in a corresponding change in behavior. Given this and other conflicting results we must conclude that we currently do not have a real grasp of the development of gender roles in older adulthood. (p. 261-262)

3. Jung proposed two major age-related trends in personality development in adulthood. First, he believed that young adults were more extroverted and older adults became more introverted. He also theorized that all humans possess elements of masculinity and femininity. In our youth, we express one element while actively suppressing the other. As adults, we begin to allow the suppressed element to surface. This ultimately results in a balance of masculine and feminine elements in older adulthood. (p. 263-264)

4. Erik Erikson's personality model contained a total of eight stages. The first four dealt with infancy through childhood. The final four dealt with development from adolescence through old age. Stage 5 (identity versus identity confusion) occurs during adolescence and involves the major crisis of "finding one's self." In this stage, peers and role models have a great impact on an individual's thoughts and actions. Stage 6 (intimacy versus isolation) occurs during young adulthood. This crisis involves the establishment of a love relationship. Stage 7 (generativity versus stagnation) is the major crisis of middle-adulthood. The key here involves the development of the capacity to assist the next generation through activities such as parenting or teaching. Stage 8 (integrity versus despair) is found in old age. With one's growing awareness of impending death, it is critical for a person to conduct a life review and conclude that life was full and meaningful. (p. 256-266)

5. Van Geert argued that movement from one Eriksonian stage to the next occurs in three steps: (a) an inward orientation to self replaces an outward orientation toward the world; (b) movement from use of general to specific categories; and (c) movement from a limited to an expanded conceptualization of experience. (p. 267)

6. Loevinger saw ego development in adults as progressing through six stages: (a) conformist (marked by absolute conformity to societal rules); (b) conscientious-conformist (the separation of personal goals and society norms); (c) conscientious (the setting of self-determined goals and ideals); (d) individualistic (the realization of the importance of individuality resulting in a differentiation between process and outcome); (e) autonomous (extreme respect of individuality and acceptance of tolerance); and (f) integrated (resolution of inner conflict). (p. 268-270)

7. The three postulates proposed by Thomae in his cognitive theory of personality development were (a) perception change is more related to behavioral change than objective change; (b) people perceive and evaluate change in terms of their current dominant concerns; and (c) adjustment to aging is determined by a balance between cognitive and motivational structures. (p. 273-274)

8. Whitbourne built a personality model on the premise that individuals have a conception of how one's life should be and attempt to use internal and external sources of information to validate this conception. She believes that we each develop a life-span construct based on scenarios (our expectations of the future) and life stories (our personal narrative that helps organize our past). As we go through life, we attempt to reconcile our scenarios with our life stories. To accomplish this, we utilize identity accommodation (the use of situational factors in self-evaluation) and identity assimilation (the use of already established aspects of identity to deal with new situations). Life transitions occur only when a person feels the need to change. (p. 275-277)

9. Kohlberg hypothesized that moral reasoning takes place at the following three levels: (a) preconventional level (judgment is based on personal gain or loss); (b) conventional level (judgment is based on societal rules or beliefs); and (c) postconventional (judgment is based on universal principles that transcend culture and time). (p. 281-284)

10. Gilligan argued that Kohlberg had created a sexist model because males tend to score at stage 4 and females tend to score at stage 3. She suggested that the difference was the result of women's orientation toward responsibilities and relationships (reflected in stage 3--mutual interpersonal conformity) and men's orientation toward justice (reflected in stage 4--social system and conscience). (p. 284-286)

IV. AFTER THE FACTS

1. Think about an older person that you have known over a long period of time. What personality characteristics appear to have been stable over that time? What characteristics have changed?

2. Given your new knowledge concerning factors that may influence life satisfaction in old age and your "current personality," what kind of life review might you expect to make when you are elderly? Speculate on upcoming life events that may alter your later life review.

3. Cognitive theorists believe that what you think you did or are is more important than what you actually have done or who you really are. Given this, what advice might you give to someone taking care of a person with Alzheimer's?

4. Think about your beliefs concerning any controversial issues (e.g., gun control, abortion, euthanasia, capital punishment). In which of Kohlberg's stages of moral thinking are you operating for each issue?

V. REVIEW ANSWERS

Terms to Know
Check the Key Terms section for Chapter 8 (p. 288-289)

True/False Answers
1. False (p.253)   6. False (p.268)
2. False (p.257)   7. False (p.271-272)
3. True (p.259)   8. True (p.273)
4. False (p.261)   9. False (p.279)
5. True (p.266)   10. True (p.284)

Fill-in-the-Blank(s) Answers
1. trait (p. 255)
2. extraversion (p. 256)
3. passive (p. 259)
4. ego (p. 263)
5. epigenetic (p. 264)
6. integrated (p. 269-270); resolve interpersonal conflicts (p. 260-270)
7. the scenario (p. 275); the life story (p. 276)
8. Self-concept (p. 277)
9. Personal control (p. 279)
10. universal ethical principles (p. 283)

Multiple Choice Answers
1. C (p.253-254)   9. B (p.262-263)   17. B (p.274)
2. D (p.255)   10. C (p.263)   18. D (p.277)
3. C (p.256-257)   11. A (p.264-265)   19. D (p.277-278)
4. B (p.257)   12. B (p.265-266)   20. B (p.278-279)
5. C (p.257-258)   13. A (p.266-267)   21. C (p.280)
6. A (p.259)   14. A (p.268-269)   22. C (p.282-283)
7. A (p.260)   15. B (p.270)   23. D (p.285-286)
8. B (p.261)   16. C (p.272)   24. B (p.286-287)

CHAPTER 9
PSYCHOPATHOLOGY AND TREATMENT

I. PREVIEW

Focus Questions

☞ **What causes depression and how do you treat it?**
(Focus on: Causes of Depression; Treatment of Depression)

☞ **Do suicide rates increase with age?**
(Focus on: Suicide)

☞ **How do you detect and treat Alzheimer's disease?**
(Focus on: Alzheimer's Disease)

☞ **What types of dementia (other than Alzheimer's) are common in adulthood?**
(Focus on: Parkinson's Disease; Pick's Disease; Creutzfeld-Jakob Disease; Huntington's Disease)

☞ **Can dementia patients be cared for at home?**
(Focus on: Caring for Dementia Patients at Home)

☞ **How are dementia patients cared for in institutions?**
(Focus on: Working with the Institutionalized Elderly)

Chapter 9: PSYCHOPATHOLOGY AND TREATMENT

Chapter Outline

Chapter 9: PSYCHOPATHOLOGY AND TREATMENT

Chapter 9: PSYCHOPATHOLOGY AND TREATMENT

Special Sections
Something to Think About
How Do We Know?

II. REVIEW

Terms to Know

Write your own brief definition for each of the following terms.

Adult Day Care:

Alzheimer's Disease:

Amyloid:

Autosomal Dominant:

Behavior Therapy:

Benzodiazepines:

Bipolar Disorder:

Cognitive Therapy:

Delirium:

Dementia:

Dysphoria:

Heterocyclic Antidepressants (HCAs):

MAO Inhibitors:

Mental Status Exam:

Multi-Infarct Dementia:

Parkinson's Disease:

Psychoanalytic Therapy:

Respite Care:

Sundowning:

True/False Questions

    ___ 1. Dementia is a normal result of aging.

    ___ 2. Older adults have a significantly higher rate of severe depression than younger adults.

    ___ 3. The Geriatric Depression Scale (GDS) focuses only on the physical aspects of elderly depression.

    ___ 4. In some cases, severe depression may need to be treated with electroconvulsive therapy.

    ___ 5. Eating cheddar cheese or chicken liver while using MAO inhibitors to treat depression may result in death.

    ___ 6. The rate of suicide among persons 65 and older increased significantly between 1962 and 1980.

    ___ 7. More than 50 percent of people over age 65 suffer from some form of dementia.

    ___ 8. Only an autopsy can provide a definitive diagnosis of Alzheimer's disease.

    ___ 9. Many individuals with Down's syndrome develop Alzheimer's-like symptoms during middle adulthood.

    ___ 10. Daughters are far more likely than sons to care for an elderly parent.

Fill-in-the-Blank(s) Questions

1. An accurate assessment of abnormality in behavior must take into consideration the _____ in which the behavior occurs.

2. The high rate of depression found in middle-age males appears to be strongly related to the high incidence of _____.

3. The cause of depression falls into one of two general categories, _____ and _____.

4. Freud used the term _____ to refer to the concept of depression being hostility turned inward.

5. A person suffering bouts of severe depression and extreme mania is said to have a _____ affect disorder.

6. _____ like Valium or Librium are commonly prescribed for treatment of anxiety disorders.

7. The key to paranoia appears to involve a well-formed _____.

8. _____ is the most common form of progressive dementia accounting for about _____ of all dementia cases.

9. Multi-infarct dementia occurs as the result of numerous _____ (strokes).

10. _____ is designed to provide caregivers the opportunity to get some time away from the person they are caring for.

Multiple Choice Questions

1. _____ is considered normal for many older adults, but abnormal for young adults.
   A. Isolation   C. Passivity
   B. Aggressiveness   D. all of the above

2. Which of the following is **not** an intrapersonal factor that may influence behavior?
   A. cognitive abilities   C. age
   B. relationship with spouse D. gender

3. Which statement concerning clinical assessment is **false**?
   A. The DSM III-R does not provide different lists of mental disorders based on the age of an individual.
   B. Few tests have been standardized on an elderly population.
   C. Most clinical measures have been developed for older adults but are being used to test younger adults.
   D. Rigid time schedules may artificially inflate the incidence of "abnormality" in older adults.

4. Researchers estimate that about _____ of adults over age 60 suffer from severe depression.
   A. 1%   C. 21%
   B. 11%   D. 51%

5. In the U.S., the number of severely depressed men is greater than the number of severely depressed women during
   A. adulthood.   C. old age.
   B. middle adulthood.   D. all stages of life.

6. _____ are present in clinical depression but absent in "the depletion syndrome of the elderly."
   A. Feelings of worthlessness   C. Loss of interest
   B. Feelings of guilt   D. Physical symptoms

7. Biological theories concerning the cause of depression include all the following **except**
   A. neurotransmitter imbalance.
   B. an impaired right hemisphere of the brain.
   C. cerebrovascular and cardiovascular diseases.
   D. a defective 23rd chromosome.

8. Negative life events
   A. cause severe depressive episodes.
   B. may be related to the incidence of severe depressive episodes.
   C. are unrelated to the incidence of severe depressive episodes.

9. Which psychosocial theme concerning the cause of depression is most associated with the cognitive approach?
   A. loss
   B. internalization
   C. internal belief systems
   D. negative life events

10. Heterocyclic antidepressants (HCAs) are
    A. the most common depression medication.
    B. effective about 70 percent of the time.
    C. dangerous for older people taking antihypertensive medication.
    D. all of the above

11. Electroconvulsive therapy (ECT)
    A. is more dangerous than HCA therapy for older adults with heart problems.
    B. produces an epileptic-like seizure in the patient.
    C. is often vividly remembered by the patient undergoing treatment.
    D. all of the above

12. Reminiscence and life review therapies are commonly used by
    A. psychoanalytic therapists.
    B. behavioral therapists.
    C. cognitive therapists.
    D. implosive therapists.

13. The highest rate of suicide would be found among older
    A. white males.
    B. Hispanic males.
    C. African-American males.
    D. Asian males.

14. Which statement concerning anxiety disorders is **true**?
    A. Anxiety disorders are less common than severe depression in older populations.
    B. Physical symptoms of anxiety disorders can include sweating, dizziness, headaches and/or chest pain.
    C. Psychotherapeutic techniques have been found to be ineffective in the treatment of anxiety in older populations.
    D. all of the above

15. Research has shown that older schizophrenics tend to have delusions concerning
    A. sex.   C. religion.
    B. aliens.   D. food.

16. Dementias
    A. are characterized by cognitive and behavioral deficits resulting from brain damage.
    B. are often classified as presenile or senile, because age appears to play a large role in the underlying neurological changes.
    C. cannot be reversed.
    D. all of the above

17. New research has indicated that Alzheimer's disease may be caused by a decrease in _____, a marker for _____.
    A. choline acetyltransferase; acetylcholine
    B. L-Dopa; dopamine
    C. Serafras; seratonin
    D. globulineoxide; GABA

18. The fact that symptoms of Alzheimer's often worsen during a particular time of the day has given rise to the term
    A. dawning.   C. sundowning.
    B. nooning.   D. midnighting.

19. Which item would appear on a mental status exam?
    A. Who is president?   C. What day is it?
    B. Can you count to 100?   D. all of the above

20. Which of the following was **not** listed as a criteria for the diagnosis of probable Alzheimer's disease?
    A. seizures
    B. no disturbance of consciousness
    C. onset after age 55
    D. family history of similar disorders

21. An autosomal dominant gene pattern means that
    A. only one gene from either parent is necessary to produce the disease.
    B. only a gene from your father can produce the disease.
    C. only a gene from your mother can produce the disease.
    D. specific genes from both parents are necessary to produce the disease.

22. Drugs used to treat Alzheimer's patients include all of the following **except**
    A. antidepressants.   C. sedatives.
    B. "memory" drugs.   D. lithium.

23. _____ appears to be transmitted by a virus.
    A. Normal-pressure hydrocephalus
    B. Huntington's disease
    C. Pick's disease
    D. Creutzfeld-Jakob disease

24. _____ is an interesting disorder because its symptoms closely resemble Alzheimer's disease, but its accompanying neurological changes are very different.
    A. Normal-pressure hydrocephalus
    B. Huntington's disease
    C. Pick's disease
    D. Creutzfeld-Jakob disease

25. Family therapists assume that
    A. functional families work toward the growth and development of their members.
    B. changing the behavior of one family member results in a change to the entire family system.
    C. communication skills training is critical to effective communication within the family.
    D. all of the above

26. _____ is designed to encourage a person to believe something that is not true.
    A. Remotivation therapy   C. Reality orientation
    B. Validation therapy   D. Milieu therapy

27. A nursing home resident would have the most input into the structure of a _____ program.
    A. remotivation therapy   C. reality orientation
    B. validation therapy   D. milieu therapy

III. SHORT-ANSWER ESSAY (QUESTIONS AND ANSWERS)

Questions

1. Identify the six characteristics of mentally healthy people proposed by Birren and Renner.

2. Briefly describe the DSM III-R criteria for a Major Depressive Episode (MDE).

3. What are the major potential causes of depression proposed by psychosocial theorists?

4. Compare and contrast behavior, cognitive, and psychoanalytic therapy approaches to depression.

5. Briefly summarize age, gender, and ethnic differences in suicide rates.

6. Describe the three common prognoses to people experiencing a schizophrenic episode.

7. What are the basic structural changes that occur in the brain of an Alzheimer's patient?

8. Briefly describe the progression of Alzheimer's disease.

9. Identify the major theories concerning the cause of Alzheimer's disease.

10. Compare and contrast multi-infarct dementia, Parkinson's disease, and Huntington's disease.

11. Discuss the issue of caregiver burden.

12. Compare and contrast different types of intervention techniques commonly used when working with institutionalized older adults.

Answers

1. Birren and Renner stated that mentally healthy people have (a) a positive self-attitude; (b) an accurate perception of reality; (c) a mastery of their environment; (d) automony; (e) personality balance; and (f) self-actualization. (p. 293)

2. The DSM III-R criteria for a Major Depressive Episode include (a) dysphoric mood (feeling pessimistic or helpless); (b) related symptoms (e.g., insomnia, changes in appetite, loss of interest in activities); (c) symptoms last at least two weeks; (d) symptoms not caused by a known health, medication, or organic problem; and (e) symptoms must impact daily activity. (p. 296-298)

3. Psychosocial theorists focus on four possible causes of depression. The most common theme involves a personal loss (e.g., life style, failure of a plan, status, loved one). Other researchers focus on negative life events (e.g., bad day at work). A third theme involves the Freudian concept of internalization that occurs when we focus our displeasure toward others onto ourselves. A final theme concerns the development of faulty internal belief systems based on our misinterpretation of life events, which allows for the development of a feeling of helplessness. (p. 300-301)

4. The basic premise of behavior therapy is that depression results when people receive too few rewards from their environment. The key to treatment involves increasing a person's activity level to improve their odds of having something good happen. Cognitive therapy views depression as the result of having improper beliefs about oneself. People are taught to form new attributions and to change the basic problematic thoughts. Psychotherapy involves having the patient gain insight into defense mechanisms responsible for their problems and then develop alternative mechanisms for dealing with the problems. (p. 303-304)

5. Rates of suicide vary greatly by age, gender, and ethnic group. Age related data shows that people over age 65 have the highest overall rate of suicide. They also have the highest attempts-to-successes ratio. Females are found to attempt suicide more often than males; however, males are significantly more successful. Data from studies of ethnic differences shows that whites are significantly more likely to commit suicide than other ethnic groups. (p. 306)

6. The three prognoses are as follows: (a) Some experience only one episode and never have a reoccurance. (b) Others display symptoms over an extended period of time, but gradually display no symptoms. (c) Some individuals have constant symptoms for the rest of their lives. (p. 308)

7. Alzheimer's disease is characterized by three changes within the brain: (a) neurofibrillary tangles (the accumulation of pairs of filaments in the neuron that wrap around one another); (b) neuritic plaques (the accumulation of dead or dying neurons around a core amyloid); and (c) granulovacuolar degeneration (the filling of brain vacuoles with fluid and granular material). There is also some evidence of brain atrophy. (p. 312)

8. The exact progression of Alzheimer's varies by subject; however, the typical progression is as follows: (a) normal state; (b) forgetfulness (minor memory loss typically for names or location of objects); (c) early confusional (significant increase in memory loss for names, location, and recent events and a loss in concentration); (d) late confusional (decrease in knowledge of current or recent events, beginning of memory deficit for personal history); (e) early dementia (distortion of time and place, difficulty in performing common activities); (f) middle dementia (severe memory loss, delusions, paranoia, obsessive behaviors); and (g) late dementia (verbal abilities lost, loss of psychomotor abilities). (p. 314-316)

9. Theories on the potential cause of Alzheimer's include (a) a slow acting viral infection; (b) aluminium toxicity; and (c) genetic disorder with an autosomal dominant pattern. (p. 318)

10. Multi-infarct dementia is caused by a series of cerebral vascular accidents ("strokes"), which result in the destruction of brain tissue. Because of its nature, multi-infarct dementia has a sudden onset and unpredictable "stuttering" progression and results in a quick death (average of 2 to 3 years). Parkinson's disease appears to be caused by a bacteria and results in several motor-related problems (e.g., slow walking, stiffness, tremors). Huntington's disease is an autosomal disease that results in several physical (e.g., repetitious motor movements) and psychological problems (e.g., hallucinations, mood swings, paranoia). (p. 321-323)

11. Caregiver burden results from the stresses involved in caring for a highly dependent adult. Some negative caregiver burden effects include (a) anger; (b) depression; (c) loss of friends; (d) financial loss; and (e) physical and mental strain. (p. 325-326)

12. Commonly used intervention techniques include (a) sensory training (focus on regaining sensory awareness utilizing body-awareness exercises and sensory stimulation); (b) reality orientation (used to reorient a patient to the current time and place they are residing); (c) validation therapy (reinforcing whatever beliefs a patient holds about themselves); (d) remotivation therapy (key is to reawaken interest in unresponsive or apathetic patients); (e) recreational therapy (focus on group activities and involvement); (f) milieu therapy (has the resident assist in designing a program best suited to their particular needs); and (g) pet therapy (use a pet to enhance responsibility, and promote social interactions). (p. 329-331)

IV. AFTER THE FACTS

1. In recent years, suicide rates for older adults have fallen whereas rates for younger adults have risen. Given your knowledge of the factors related to suicide, what pattern do you expect to emerge in the next 20 years?

2. If a test to screen for all forms of dementia existed but cures were not available, would you have yourself tested? If yes, when? What would be the advantages and disadvantages of knowing?

3. How do you think family therapy would work for your family? What factors might make it effective or ineffective?

4. If you had an elderly parent in need of in-home care, would you be willing to provide such care? What factors might influence your decision?

V. REVIEW ANSWERS

Terms to Know
Check the Key Terms section for Chapter 9 (p. 334)

True/False Answers
1. False (p.292)	6. False (p.305)
2. False (p.295)	7. False (p.309)
3. False (p.299)	8. True (p.313)
4. True (p.301)	9. True (p.318)
5. True (p.302)	10. True (p.325)

Fill-in-the-Blank(s) Answers
1. context (p. 293)
2. alcoholism (p. 295)
3. biological (physiological) (p. 299); psychosocial (p. 299)
4. internalization (p. 300-301)
5. bipolar (p. 302)
6. Benzodiazepines (p. 307)
7. delusion (p. 308)
8. Alzheimer's disease (p. 310); 70 percent (p. 310)
9. cerebral vascular accidents (CVAs) (p. 321)
10. Respite care (p. 324)

Multiple Choice Answers
1. D (p.293)	10. D (p.301-302)	19. D (p.316)
2. B (p.293-294)	11. B (p.302-303)	20. C (p.317)
3. C (p.294-295)	12. A (p.304)	21. A (p.318)
4. A (p.295)	13. A (p.306)	22. D (p.319-320)
5. B (p.295)	14. B (p.306-307)	23 D (p.322)
6. B (p.299)	15. A (p.308)	24. C (p.322)
7. D (p.299-300)	16. A (p.310)	25. D (p.327-328)
8. B (p.300)	17. A (p.312)	26. B (p.330)
9. C (p.301)	18. C (p.313)	27. D (p.331)

CHAPTER 10
RELATIONSHIPS

I. PREVIEW

Focus Questions

☞ **How do friendships change in adulthood?**
(Focus on: Friendships)

☞ **How can you define love?**
(Focus on: Love Relationships)

☞ **Does marital satisfaction change over time?**
(Focus on: Marriage)

☞ **In what ways does divorce affect adult behavior?**
(Focus on: Divorce and Remarriage)

☞ **What roles do parents play?**
(Focus on: The Parental Role)

☞ **In what ways does being a member of the sandwich generation affect one's life?**
(Focus on: Family Dynamics and Middle Age)

☞ **What roles do grandparents play?**
(Focus on: Styles of Grandparenting)

Chapter 10: RELATIONSHIPS

Chapter Outline

Special Sections
How Do We Know?
Something to Think About

II. REVIEW

Terms to Know
Write your own brief definition for each of the following terms.

Cohabitation:

Homogamy:

Kinkeepers:

Postparental Family:

Sandwich Generation:

True/False Questions

___ 1. Middle-age adults have the largest number of friends.

___ 2. Most long-term love relationships are eventually characterized by great intimacy and commitment and less passion.

___ 3. While "opposites may attract" in a longer-term relationship it appears that eventually mostly "birds of a feather flock together."

___ 4. Estimates are that more than 90 percent of Americans will marry at least once.

___ 5. Highly educated women are more likely to remain single.

___ 6. After being in a relationship for many years, the sexual behavior between gay men declines significantly.

___ 7. Half of all U.S. women over age 65 are widows.

___ 8. Nearly two-thirds of U.S. mothers with children under age six are employed.

___ 9. About 40 percent of divorced people in their twenties live with their parents.

___ 10. In the U.S., most elderly parents do not see their adult children on a regular basis.

Fill-in-the-Blank(s) Questions

1. Men tend to form friendships on the basis of _____.
2. Sternberg used the term _____ to refer to an ideal love relationship based on commitment, intimacy, and passion.
3. Buss found the greatest cross-cultural variability involved the importance of _____ in mate selection.
4. _____ refers to the belief that similarity of interests and values is critical to marital success.
5. The term _____ is used to describe a situation where two or more unmarried adults live together.
6. Internationally, the peak time for divorce is after _____ years of marriage.
7. Currently, about one in _____ American couples experience fertility problems.
8. Fathers' interactions with babies tend to involve _____ rather than caregiving.
9. When the last child is launched from a family, it creates a(n) _____ family. In the past, this has been called the _____ syndrome.
10. The term _____ is used to refer to a person who helps keep a family together through the organization of family gatherings.

Chapter 10: RELATIONSHIPS

Multiple Choice Questions

1. Which statement concerning friendship development is **false**?
   A. Opposite sex friendships in middle-age may be perceived as threats to marital status.
   B. Older adults' life satisfaction is highly related to the quality of contact with one's own family members.
   C. Friendships are important in all ethnic populations.
   D. The quality and quantity of friendships is a good predictor of life satisfaction in old-age.

2. Women tend to
   A. be more likely to reveal weakness to their friends.
   B. base friendships on emotional sharing.
   C. discuss more personal matters with their friends.
   D. all of the above

3. Which statement concerning sibling friendships is **true**?
   A. Geographic distance plays no role in the quality of sibling friendships.
   B. African-American sibling relationships tend to be very strong.
   C. Brothers tend to be stronger friends than sisters.
   D. Brothers and sisters tend to have poor relationships.

4. According to Sternberg, romantic love lacks
   A. intimacy.   C. passion.
   B. commitment.   D. nothing.

5. The most important component of love for all adults appears to be
   A. loyality.   C. communication.
   B. sexual intimacy.   D. emotional security.

6. In selecting a mate, men tend to
   A. be quicker to see a woman as a compatible mate.
   B. believe more in "love at first sight."
   C. view love as "magical and impossible to understand."
   D. all of the above

7. Individuals who marry in their teens or early twenties
   _____ those who marry after their early twenties.
   A. are more likely to get a divorce than
   B. are less likely to get a divorce than
   C. have similar divorce rates to

8. Which statement concerning marital satisfaction is **false**?
   A. Marital satisfaction typically bottoms out in midlife.
   B. Childless couples have higher marital satisfaction.
   C. Launching of the last child typically has a devastating effect on women, which results in lower marital satisfaction.
   D. A majority of persons married for fifty years did not list their spouse as one of their closest friends.

9. In older adults, _____ appears to be unrelated to marital satisfaction.
   A. health
   B. past or present sexual activity level
   C. career status
   D. none of the above

10. Weishaus and Field's longitudinal study of long-term marriages found that
    A. expectations concerning marriage become congruent with time.
    B. women are significantly more pleased with marriage.
    C. most couples experience decline in satisfaction with age.
    D. serious illness is extremely detrimental to overall satisfaction.

11. The number of single twenty-year-olds has
    A. increased significantly in the past few decades.
    B. decreased significantly in the past few decades.
    C. remained constant over the past few decades.

12. Cohabitation has
    A. increased significantly in the past few decades.
    B. decreased significantly in the past few decades.
    C. remained constant over the past few decades.

13. High numbers of cohabitants are found among
    A. college-age people.   C. women in their twenties.
    B. recent immigrants.   D. all of the above

14. Lesbian couples
    A. are highly likely to engage in sex early in a relationship.
    B. tend to have multiple partners.
    C. are more likely to stay together than a gay male couple.
    D. all of the above

15. Which statement concerning divorce is **false**?
    A. African Americans are more likely than whites to divorce.
    B. Couples marrying before age twenty are more likely to divorce.
    C. The divorce rate increased dramatically during the late 1980s.
    D. Protestants have higher divorce rates than Catholics.

16. Which of the following was found in a 1948 study to be a major
    reason given by women for divorce, but which did not even appear
    in the top ten reasons given on a 1985 report?
    A. alcohol abuse   C. cruelty or physical abuse
    B. nonsupport   D. financial problems

17. Which statement concerning the impact of divorce is **true**?
    A. Childless couples adjust better to a divorce.
    B. Women are more seriously affected by divorce.
    C. The longer a couple was married the greater the trauma.
    D. all of the above

18. Research on remarriage has shown all of the following **except**
    A. nearly 80 percent of divorced persons remarry within three years.
    B. most remarried people experience improved communication and a more equitable division of labor in the second marriage.
    C. female children tend to be more accepting of a stepparent.
    D. Remarriage later in life tends to be happier.

19. Rossi's summary of important sources of stress that accompany parenthood included
    A. possible unplanned parenthood.
    B. a lack of education for parenting.
    C. the irrevocability of having a child.
    D. all of the above

20. Which statement concerning single parents is **false**?
    A. Single parents tend to be worse off financially than married parents.
    B. Single parents indicate a great concern over their dating behavior.
    C. Women appear to be significantly more affected emotionally than men.
    D. Single parents may see children as a hindrance to the development of new relationships.

21. Research on the empty nest indicates that
    A. the return to the home of a launched child typically has a positive effect on the parents.
    B. marital satisfaction typically increases after the last child is launched.
    C. most mothers are initially devastated following the launching of the last child.
    D. all of the above

22. The term _____ generation is used to describe middle-aged people dealing with both their older parents and their adult children.
    A. "tween"   C. sandwich
    B. lost   D. parallax

23. Most older adults needing care
    A. receive it from their children or other relatives.
    B. do not financially burden other family members.
    C. have little desire to pay professionals for assistance.
    D. are extremely satisfied with the quality of care they receive.

24. "Surrogate children"
    A. are hired by middle-age children to care for their parents.
    B. can be funded by most health insurance programs.
    C. are significantly cheaper than the cost of placing an adult in a nursing home.
    D. all of the above

25. Most U.S. grandparents under age 65 have a _____ grandparenting style.
    A. formal   C. fun-seeking
    B. distant   D. symbolic

26. Detachment between grandparents and other family members appears to be the result of
    A. increased geographic mobility.
    B. grandparent employment.
    C. the high divorce rate.
    D. all of the above

27. Which was **not** one of the key aspects of great-grandparenthood identified by Doka and Mertz?
    A. It provides a sense of personal renewal.
    B. Symbolic immortality helps them face death.
    C. It provides another child-rearing opportunity.
    D. It is a longevity milestone.

III. SHORT-ANSWER ESSAY (QUESTIONS AND ANSWERS)

Questions

1. Describe the stages in friendship development.

2. Briefly discuss factors that lead to a decrease in the number of friends found between young adulthood and old age.

3. Identify and describe the components of of Sternberg's theory of love.

4. Briefly describe Murstein's stages of mate selection.

5. Describe the general developmental pattern of marital satisfaction.

6. List some similarities between cohabitants and married couples.

7. Differentiate between the main reasons for divorce given by men and those given by women.

8. Why do women appear to be more affected by divorce?

9. Describe Lopata's six reactions to widowhood.

10. Robinson and Thurnher found that stress in caregiving for an elderly parent typically occurred for one of two reasons. Describe them.

11. Compare and contrast Neugarten and Weinstein's grandparenting styles with the alternative proposed by Robertson.

12. Describe Kivnick's five meanings of grandparenting.

Answers

1. Friendships appear to be formed in a three-stage process: (a) mutual awareness (initial notice and superficial judgements); (b) surface contact (more interaction but behavior governed by existing social norms); and (c) true friendship (characterized by self-disclosure and commitment). (p. 338)

2. Factors that lead younger people to have more friends than older people include: (a) College-age people often have access to a large pool of potential friends; as they leave school, the number of people they encounter is reduced resulting in a diminished number of potential friends. (b) Geographic movement in adulthood often disrupts friendships. (c) Family and career obligations begin to take precedence over friendship formation. (d) Opposite sex friendships diminish as they become a potential threat to marriage status. (e) As we get older, the friends that we have will begin to die. (p. 338-339)

3. Sternberg believes that love consisted of three basic components: (a) passion (physiological desire); (b) intimacy (the desire to share thoughts and actions); and (c) commitment (the desire to stay with a person despite hardships). He combined these basic components to create seven specific forms of love: (a) liking (intimacy only); (b) infatuation (passion only); (c) empty love (commitment only); (d) romantic love (intimacy and passion); (e) fatuous love (commitment and passion); (f) companionate love (commitment and intimacy); and (g) consummate love (passion, commitment, and intimacy). (p. 340-341)

4. Murstein hypothesized that mate selection typically occurs in a three-stage process: (a) interesting stimuli (initial attraction is based on some basic characteristic of the individual--often appearance or status); (b) comparison of values (initial discussion of attitudes toward issues like marriage, politics, values); and (c) intimate comparison (as roles develop within a relationship individuals check on the specific day-to-day behaviors of their potential mate). (p. 341-342)

5. Research on the pattern of marital satisfaction has revealed a strikingly similar developmental progression. Satisfaction appears to be highest during the first year or so of marriage (honeymoon phase). As the honeymoon bliss wanes, a drop in marital satisfaction is noted. This decline is often accelerated by the birth of the first child. Satisfaction bottoms out during midlife as teen children and/or career issues compete with the couple's relationship. There is often an increase in satisfaction following the launching of the last child. Data on later marriage satisfaction is mixed with factors like health and work status being better predictors than the length of time married. (p. 344-347)

6. Though the prevailing attitude is that cohabitants are very different from those who marry, in reality the two groups are quite similar. For example, both groups have similar ideas concerning division of labor, communication, finances, fidelity within the relationship, and the view that cohabitation is not a replacement for marriage. (p. 349-350)

7. Surprisingly, the reasons for divorce given by men and women are not very different. Cleek and Pearson found that males' top ten answers included (a) communication problems; (b) basic unhappiness; (c) incompatibility; (d) sexual problems; (e) financial problems; (f) emotional abuse; (g) women's liberation; (h) in-laws; (i) infidelity by spouse; and (j) alcohol abuse by self. The list for females was virtually identical, with just a few changes in order: (a) communication problems; (b) basic unhappiness; (c) incompatibility; (d) emotional abuse; (e) financial problems; (f) sexual problems; (g) alcohol abuse by spouse; (h) infidelity by spouse; (i) physical abuse; and (j) in-laws. (p. 351-352)

8. Although divorce has an impact on both men and women, women appear to be especially at risk because of the following factors: (a) Financial changes including loss of spouse's income, and child care costs. (b) Loss in status as wife. (c) Middle- and older-age women are less likely to remarry. (p. 353)

9. Lapota identified six patterns of widowhood: (a) "liberated" (person had worked through the trauma following the death of her spouse; (b) "merry widow" (funfilled life style); (c) working women (highly career oriented); (d) "widow's widows" (lived alone, valued independence, and associated with other widows); (e) traditional widow (lived with children and were active mothers and grandmothers); and (f) grieving widow (isolated and unable to work through the death of their husbands). (p. 355-356)

10. Robinson and Thurnher saw stress in caregiving as the result of (a) having trouble coping with the mental decline of the parent; or (b) the perception of the caregiving relationship as restricting the behaviors of the adult child. (p. 363)

11. In 1964, Neugarten and Weinstein identified five types of grandparenting styles: (a) formal (strong interest in grandchildren but hands-off attitude toward child rearing); (b) fun seeker (focus on play activities); (c) distant (little contact other than during formal occasions); (d) surrogate parents (filling in for working parents); and (e) dispenser of family wisdom (typically an authoritarian grandfather). Robertson (1977) developed a model based on personal factors and individual need. She identified four grandparent types: (a) appointed (highly involved and concerned about indulgence and moral development); (b) remote (detached and few expectations about grandparent role); (c) symbolic (few role expectations but emphasized normative and moral aspects of behavior); and (d) individualized (emphasis on the personal aspects of grandparenting while ignoring the social role). (p. 365)

12. Kivnick's five meanings of grandparenting are as follows: (a) centrality (the degree to which grandparenting is primary to one's life); (b) value as an elder (perception of being wise or helpful); (c) immortality through clan (having left behind two generations); (d) reinvolvement in one's personal past (recall of relationships with one's own grandparents); and (e) indulgence (pleasure from giving to grandchildren). (p. 366)

IV. AFTER THE FACTS

1. Reflect back upon your first "true love." In which of Sternberg's categories would this love have best fit? Have most of your subsequent loves fit this same category? Have you ever experienced consummate love?

2. Given the data concerning divorce, singlehood, remarriage, and our society's current concern over the importance of a two-parent family system, would you be more in favor of restricting divorce or encouraging remarriage following divorce? What other "solutions" to this social issue can you generate?

3. Would you care for your parents if they became severely disabled or demented? What factors might influence your decision?

4. If you still have or can remember having had grandparents, what grandparenting style did they appear to use? Did their interaction style change as you and they aged?

V. REVIEW ANSWERS

Terms to Know
Check the Key Terms section for Chapter 10 (p. 371)

True/False Answers

1. False (p.338)	6. True (p.350)
2. True (p.341)	7. True (p.355)
3. True (p.342)	8. True (p.357)
4. True (p.344)	9. True (p.361)
5. True (p.347-348)	10. False (p.362)

Fill-in-the-Blank(s) Answers
1. shared activities or interests (p. 339)
2. consummate (p. 341)
3. chastity (p. 343)
4. Homogamy (p. 344)
5. cohabitation (p. 348)
6. three to four (p. 351)
7. six (p. 357)
8. play (p. 357)
9. post-parental (p. 360); empty-nest (p. 360)
10. kinkeeper (p. 361)

Multiple Choice Answers

1. B (p.338-339)	10. A (p.347)	19. D (p.357)
2. D (p.339)	11. A (p.347)	20. C (p.359)
3. B (p.339-340)	12. A (p.348)	21. B (p.360-361)
4. B (p.340)	13. D (p.349)	22. C (p.361)
5. D (p.341-342)	14. C (p.350)	23. A (p.363-364)
6. D (p.342)	15. C (p.351)	24. A (p.364)
7. A (p.344)	16. B (p.351-352)	25. C (p.365)
8. C (p.345-346)	17. D (p.353)	26. D (p.367-368)
9. B (p.346)	18. C (p.354-355)	27. C (p.368-369)

CHAPTER 11
WORK, LEISURE, AND RETIREMENT

I. PREVIEW

Focus Questions

☞ **What factors are important in making career choices?**
(Focus on: Personality and Interests; Self-Efficacy; Gender Differences)

☞ **Are there stages in occupational development?**
(Focus on: Super's Theory)

☞ **Do age and gender impact occupation?**
(Focus on: Women and Occupational Development; Age Discrimination)

☞ **Why do we change jobs?**
(Focus on: Factors Influencing Occupational Change)

☞ **Do dual-career couples experience unique problems?**
(Focus on: Handling Multiple Roles)

☞ **How do psychologists categorize leisure?**
(Focus on: Types of Leisure Activities)

☞ **Why do we retire and how do we react to retirement?**
(Focus on: Deciding to Retire; Adjustment to Retirement)

Chapter Outline

Special Sections
How Do We Know?
Something to Think About

II. REVIEW

Terms to Know
Write your own brief definition for each of the following terms.

Age Discrimination:

Comparable Worth:

Glass Ceiling:

Mentor:

Occupational Priorities:

Preretirement Educational Program:

Reality Shock:

Role Conflict:

Self-Efficacy:

Sex Discrimination:

Vocational Maturity:

True/False Questions

___　1.　Money is the primary reason why most people work.

___　2.　Self-efficacy theory predicts that people who do not believe they are good at an occupation are highly likely to "give it a shot" anyway.

___ 3. Super's theory of occupational development views occupations as static.

___ 4. Betz's study of female college graduates showed that about 25 percent had been full-time homemakers during the first ten years following graduation.

___ 5. Because of superior verbal skills, women appear to have an easier time finding a career mentor.

___ 6. The average American will change jobs between five and ten times during adulthood.

___ 7. Most dual-career couples in America equally divide child-care and household maintenance responsibilities.

___ 8. The majority of men and women agree that a couple should not move if a wife receives a great job offer but it means disrupting the husband's career.

___ 9. The 1935 Social Security Act in some ways "created" the concept of retirement.

___ 10. Individuals with a strong work orientation appear to have the hardest time with retirement.

Fill-in-the-Blank(s) Questions

1. The term _____ refers to any kind of work, whereas the term _____ is typically reserved for a job with prestige.

2. Jobs traditionally held by women are referred to as _____ occupations.

3. Super's theory of occupational development is based on the issue of _____. In this theory, people are thought to proceed along a continuum of _____ maturity.

4. The fact that traditional female jobs (nursing, teacher) pay less than traditional male jobs (construction or factory worker) leads to _____ or the problem of _____.

5. The realization that textbook examples learned in school often do not match the real world can lead to _____ shock.

6. Mentoring fulfills Erikson's psychosocial crisis of _____.

7. Shirom and Mazeh's study of job satisfaction in junior high school teachers found that satisfaction ran in _____ cycles and appeared to be relatively unrelated to age.

8. Many women experience a significant _____ conflict as they try to balance the goal of raising children with the expectation of establishing a career.

9. An important constant across the lifespan involves the _____ of the leisure activities one engages in.

10. Retired men tend to do _____ housework than they did before retirement.

Multiple Choice Questions

1. In his book <u>Working</u>, Studs Terkel states that work is a search for
   A. daily bread.   C. recognition.
   B. daily meaning.   D. all of the above

2. In the U.S., which of the following people would **not** be viewed as having a career?
   A. a psychology professor   C. an airline pilot
   B. an assembly-line worker   D. none of the above

3. Most union workers have
   A. blue-collar occupations.   C. pink-collar occupations.
   B. white-collar occupations.   D. executive occupations.

4. According to Holland, a bookkeeper or statistician most likely has a _____ personality.
   A. investigative   C. realistic
   B. conventional   D. enterprising

5. Holland would predict that a _____ would have a social personality.
   A. clinical psychologist   C. concert singer
   B. master of ceremonies   D. court stenographer

6. Barnett and Baruch's controversial findings concerning gender differences in occupation selection were that
   A. women intentionally avoid high-prestige occupations.
   B. males are given significantly less career support when they are young.
   C. women tend to overestimate their graduate school potential.
   D. all of the above

7. The "trial work period" typically occurs in the _____ stage of occupational development.
   A. implementation   C. maintenance
   B. establishment   D. declaration

8. In the U.S., women are discriminated against in
   A. hiring.   C. pay.
   B. promotion.   D. all of the above

9. Bielby and Bielby found that females with similar household responsibilities as males devoted
   A. less time to work than males.
   B. more time to work than males.
   C. the same amount of time to work as males.

10. Federal court cases on age discrimination have been shown to
    A. typically favor the employee.
    B. ban stereotypic statements made concerning older workers.
    C. use performance as a major factor.
    D. all of the above

11. Which is **not** a critical factor in the occupational success of U.S. males?
    A. number of years of formal education
    B. ethnic background
    C. intelligence
    D. marital status

12. Research on occupational expectations has shown that
    A. most young persons form a dream concerning their possible employment status.
    B. many workers encounter a shock as they realize that the real world differs from textbook examples.
    C. workers may forego promotions for family reasons.
    D. all of the above

13. The moderate increase in job satisfaction with age may be related to all of the following **except**
    A. many men appear to take more to keep satisfied.
    B. the self-selected nature of the population studied.
    C. a more realistic understanding concerning the amount of control one has in an occupation.
    D. the fact that people change jobs with which they are not satisfied.

14. _____ is **not** a good predictor of occupational change.
    A. Fear of failure   C. A history of emotional problems
    B. Age   D. A lack of diversified interests

15. Hard hit occupations in the U.S. include
    A. farming.   C. steel manufacturing.
    B. automobile manufacturing.   D. all of the above

16. Which statement concerning dual-career couples is **false**?
    A. Most couples successfully resolve the tension between family and career responsibility.
    B. Women are most satisfied with a division of labor based on an equity in the number of hours both the husband and wife spend on household chores.
    C. The extra income from the second working spouse is typically felt to be "worth the costs."
    D. Low stress in men was most prominent when they had a flexible work schedule that allowed for handling family matters.

17. A preoccupation is best thought of as being like a(n)
    A. attraction.   C. idea.
    B. feeling.   D. daydream.

18. The two most critical factors in determining the types of leisure activities we will engage in appear to be
    A. perceived competence and psychological comfort with the activity.
    B. ethnic background and gender.
    C. age and level of intelligence.
    D. income level and geographic location.

19. Which statement concerning leisure activities is **false**?
    A. Men are more likely to participate in outdoor leisure activities.
    B. Health is seldom used as a reason to exclude oneself from participation in a leisure activity.
    C. People in retirement housing participate more in leisure activity than those in a typical neighborhood.
    D. Frequent participation in an activity in childhood is a good predictor of engagement in that activity in adulthood.

20. Calculating possible retirement benefits is used as an example of retirement as a
    A. process.   C. paradox.
    B. change.   D. renewal.

21. The main reason for early retirement among whites involves
    A. health status.   C. financial status.
    B. educational level. D. personality characteristics.

22. Research on retirement satisfaction has shown that
    A. most people are generally satisfied with retirement.
    B. in recent years, more retirees have indicated a desire to work.
    C. retirees not collecting pensions were more likely to want to keep working.
    D. all of the above

23. _____ does **not** appear to be related to satisfaction among retirees.
    A. Frequency of contact with relatives
    B. Having intimate friendships
    C. Awareness of community services
    D. Marital status

24. The average person can expect a _____ reduction in income when they retire.
    A. 10%   C. 50%
    B. 25%   D. 75%

III. SHORT-ANSWER ESSAY (QUESTIONS AND ANSWERS)

Questions

1. Briefly describe five general levels of workers.

2. Identify Holland's six types of personality and related occupational choices.

3. Describe the stages in Super's theory of occupational development.

4. Discuss the concepts of sex discrimination, the glass ceiling, and comparable worth.

5. What was the four-stage mentoring sequence proposed by Kram?

6. What were the general findings from the AT&T longitudinal study of occupational priorities?

7. List some factors that influence occupational change.

8. Leisure activities can be organized in terms of the degree of personal involvement. Briefly discuss (and provide specific examples) of such an organization.

9. What factors are most critical in one's decision to retire?

10. Describe Lowenthal's classifications of work-style types and resulting reactions to retirement.

11. Describe some of the major components of a preretirement program.

Answers

1. Five general levels of workers include (a) marginal workers (work on occasion but no long-term employment pattern); (b) blue-collar occupations (have jobs not requiring a high school degree and that often rely on physical strength); (c) pink-collar (jobs traditionally held by women); (d) white-collar occupations (office-based jobs); and (e) executive and professional careers (require the highest education and result in more control over one's career development). (p. 375-376)

2. Holland's personality types are (a) investigative (task-oriented and asocial); (b) social (humanistic, verbal, high social skills); (c) realistic (physically strong, aggressive, good motor coordination skills); (d) artistic (avoids highly structured or gross physical activities, high need for individual expression); (e) conventional (prefer structured verbal or numeric activities, subordinate role); and (f) enterprising (dominating, good verbal skills for sales, great concern for power or status). (p. 378-379)

3. Super hypothesized a strong relationship between occupation and expected age-related behavior. He proposed that occupational development progressed through the following five stages: (a) implementation stage (adolescence--key is to learn first-hand about work roles and identify possible compatible occupations); (b) establishment (young adulthood--selection of a specific occupation followed by achievement and advancement within the occupation); (c) maintenance (middle-age--a diminished need to achieve); (d) deceleration (near retirement age--prepare for retirement and separate from career); and (e) retirement (post-retirement age--end full-time employment). (p. 380-381)

4. Currently, sex discrimination (denying a job solely on the basis of gender) is a major barrier to occupational development in women. Many career women may encounter a "glass ceiling" in their occupations. This artificial ceiling limits how high they can rise within a corporation. In addition to hiring and promotion discrimination, women are often the victims of pay inequity. For example, a woman will earn less for doing the same job as a man. In addition, the issue of comparable worth reveals a trend of paying typical female occupations less than traditional male occupations. (p. 382-383)

5. Kram believed that the mentor-protege relationship developed in the following progression: (a) initiation (first six to twelve months--establish an initial working relationship); (b) cultivation (two to five years--very active phase with mentor providing considerable input); (c) separation (protege emerges from protection of the mentor often through a promotion to a similar status job); and (d) redefinition (new relationship with rules based more on friendship). (p. 385)

6. The AT&T study on changes in occupational priorities found no differences between young and old workers on intellectual ability, need for achievement, or personal work standards. Differences between young and old workers did, however, emerge in the areas of motivation for upward mobility (young, higher), expectation for rewards from work (young, lower), and desire for early promotion (old, higher). Finally, ratings for the importance of work increased as one's level of management status increased. (p. 387-388)

7. Factors involved in occupational change include (a) personality (key is to have congruence between your preferences and the rewards from the occupation); (b) obsolescence (technological changes may make your occupation obsolete); and (c) economics (may not make enough money to make ends meet). (389-391)

8. Forms of leisure are often categorized by the amount of cognitive, physical, or emotional involvement. An example of a low-intensity leisure activity would be taking a nap. A moderately low activity might involve reading for pleasure. A medium-intensity activity could involve sightseeing or attending a cultural event. A moderately high-intensity leisure activity would involve participation in a creative activity (e.g., painting, singing) or serious discussion. Very high-level events would include sexual activity, dancing, or sports participation. (p. 396)

9. The decision to retire appears to be affected by numerous factors including (a) health (poor health may lead to early retirement); (b) financial status (security may lead to retirement); (c) attitude toward retirement (people with rewarding jobs may delay retirement); (d) gender (a woman's decision to retire is often based on her husband's work-related status); and (e) ethnicity (ethnic differences in retirement may be important but are currently not well defined).   (p. 399-401)

10. Lowenthal classified people as being either (a) highly work-oriented (view work as an end in itself--have a difficult time with retirement); (b) receptive-nurturant (have lifetime goal involving relationships and intimacy, provided there is a solid relationship with another person and retirement is not viewed as a problem); (c) autonomous (in occupations where they have some input into retirement--if retirement is voluntary it is no problem, if retirement is forced there can be depression); and (d) self-protective (view retirement as another life chapter--no real problem unless it leads to some significant life change). (p. 401-402)

11. Topics commonly covered in a preretirement program include (a) finances (Social Security, pension, insurance); (b) timing of retirement; (c) legal issues (wills, rights); (d) leisure activities (travel, clubs, educational opportunities, hobbies); (e) health issues (Medicare, health problems); and (f) psychological issues (work roles, effects on family, effects on personal identity). (p. 404-406)

IV. AFTER THE FACTS

1. Reflect on Holland's theory of personality and occupational choices. What careers might be best suited to "your personality?" What careers might you want to avoid?

2. Are you planning to have a one-career life or do you you plan to have several jobs in your lifetime? What would be the advantages and disadvantages of each scenario?

3. What are some of your favorite leisure activities? Do you expect to continue with these for the remainder of your life? If no, why not?

4. When do you plan to retire? How much money will you have at retirement? Where will you spend your retirement years? What activities will you engage in during your retirement years?

V. REVIEW ANSWERS

Terms to Know
Check the Key Terms section for Chapter 11 (p. 409)

True/False Answers
1. True (p.375)	6. True (p.389)
2. False (p.377-378)	7. False (p.393)
3. False (p.381)	8. True (p.394)
4. False (p.381-382)	9. True (p.397)
5. False (p.386)	10. True (p.401)

Fill-in-the-Blank(s) Answers
1. occupation (p. 375); career (p. 375)
2. pink-collar (p. 376)
3. self-concept (p. 380); vocational (p. 381)
4. sex discrimination (p. 382); comparable worth (p. 382)
5. reality (p. 384)
6. generativity (p. 385)
7. five-year (p. 390)
8. role (p. 392)
9. quality (p. 395)
10. more (p. 403)

Multiple Choice Answers
1. D (p.374)	9. B (p.382-383)	17. D (p.395)
2. B (p.375)	10. C (p.383)	18. A (p.396)
3. A (p.376)	11. D (p.383)	19. B (p.397)
4. B (p.378-379)	12. D (p.384-385)	20. A (p.398)
5. A (p.378-379)	13. A (p.387-389)	21. A (p.398-400)
6. A (p.379-380)	14. B (p.390)	22. D (p.402-403)
7. A (p.381)	15. D (p.391)	23. A (p.403-404)
8. D (p.382-383)	16. B (p.392-393)	24. C (p.405)

CHAPTER 12
WHERE WE LIVE

I. PREVIEW

Focus Questions

☞ **What is the basic premise of person-environment theories?**
(Focus on: Competence and Environmental Press; The Congruence Model)

☞ **Does community size impact life satisfaction?**
(Focus on: Community Size)

☞ **What makes for an ideal neighborhood?**
(Focus on: Neighborhoods)

☞ **What housing options are available to the elderly?**
(Focus on: Housing)

☞ **What types of health facilities are available to the elderly?**
(Focus on: Types of Institutions; Characteristics of Nursing Homes)

☞ **How do individuals adjust to relocation?**
(Focus on: Community-Based Relocation; Institutional Relocation)

Chapter 12: WHERE WE LIVE

Chapter Outline

II. REVIEW

Terms to Know
Write your own brief definition for each of the following terms.

Adaptation Level:

Competence:

Congruence Model:

Environmental Press:

Environmental Psychology:

Informal Social Network:

Loss Continuum:

Participant Observation Research:

Person-Environment Interactions:

True/False Questions

____ 1. In the Lawton and Nahemow competence-environmental press model, the more competent the person, the more impact the environment has on his or her behavior.

____ 2. The loss continuum views life as a series of losses that reduce social participation.

____ 3. Living in a city is a negative experience for the majority of older adults.

___ 4. Availability of age-peers is one of the most critical factors in determining whether an older person is satisfied with the neighborhood in which they reside.

___ 5. More than 20 percent of U.S. households are headed by a person over age 65.

___ 6. About 5 percent of homeless people are over age 60.

___ 7. A skilled nursing home provides 24-hour medical care to its residents.

___ 8. Frail elderly individuals typically see a nursing home as their first housing option.

___ 9. The most common reason for moving in people age 75 and older is retirement.

___ 10. Individuals with higher levels of education adjust better to a move.

Fill-in-the-Blank(s)   Questions

1. _____ psychology involves the study of the interaction between individuals and the community or institution in which they live.

2. _____ is the theoretical upper limit of of a person's capacity to function.

3. Schooler argued that the presence of _____ can greatly reduce the impact of environmental stressors.

4. A person's friends, neighbors, and close family members comprise their _____.

5. For African-Americans, the local _____ serves as a major source of social activity and interaction.

6. A research project in which the experimenter is actively involved within a group and reports on everyday activities of that group is using a _____ research design.

7. The goal of communities, neighborhoods, and housing should be to maximize the _____ fit.

8. The main reason for institutionalization of nursing home residents is because of their _____.

9. According to Langer's social-psychological perspective approach to the person-environment issue, the key to residents' well-being is the degree to which they _____.

10. If a move significantly improves one's _____, the benefits may be long-lasting.

Multiple Choice Questions

1. _____ is **not** part of Lewin's person-environment equation.
   A. Person   C. Environment
   B. Behavior   D. Personality

2. Person-environment theories emphasize the importance of the
   A. actual environment in which a person resides.
   B. perceived environment in which a person resides.
   C. geographic location in which a person resides.
   D. political environment in which a person resides.

3. Which is **not** one of Lawton and Nahemow's competence domains?
   A. biological   C. health
   B. ego strength   D. linguistic skills

4. Murray termed the demands that an environment places on you as environmental
   A. press.   C. limit.
   B. stress.   D. process.

5. Which statement concerning Lawton and Nahemow's competence-
   environmental press model is **true**?
   A. The adaptation level is where behavior and affect are normal.
   B. A person having too much competence in a low-press
      environment may develop maladaptive behaviors.
   C. The optimal environmental press occurs at higher levels for
      highly competent people.
   D. all of the above

6. _____is considered a "loss" according to Pastalan's loss-
   continuum approach.
   A. The death of a spouse   C. The loss of hearing
   B. Paralysis due to a stroke D. all of the above

7. Which statement concerning community size and satisfaction is
   false?
   A. When health factors are controlled, community size becomes
      nonpredictive of satisfaction.
   B. Individuals in larger cities often experience less perceived
      integration into the community.
   C. Individuals in smaller communities are more aware of available
      service for the elderly.
   D. A negative of smaller towns is there lack of transportation and
      shopping facilities.

8. _____ was **not** found by Blake and Lawton to be part of the
   definition of an "ideal community" given by the young, old, rural
   and urban.
   A. High quality medical care
   B. Low property tax
   C. An adequate number of jobs
   D. A good school system

9. Research on crime has shown that most elderly people
   A. are concerned about neighborhood crime.
   B. have been victims of crime.
   C. seldom leave their homes for fear of being crime victims.
   D. all of the above

10. _____ has the smallest number of age-segregated housing projects.
    A. The U.S.   C. France
    B. Sweden   D. Germany

11. Research on apartment complexes for the elderly have shown that
    A. racial tensions often develop.
    B. frail residents may be resented by healthy individuals.
    C. a subgroup with positive attitudes and a good sense of local relevant events may develop.
    D. all of the above

12. _____ typically consist of an apartment complex with an attached medical clinic.
    A. Congregate housing units
    B. Continuing care retirement communities
    C. SRO hotels
    D. Retirement communities

13. _____ are typically the most expensive types of housing options. In these units, an individual pays a large sum up front and then makes monthly payments.
    A. Congregate housing units
    B. Continuing care retirement communities
    C. SRO hotels
    D. Retirement communities

14. _____ SROs tend to have equal numbers of male and female occupants.
    A. Skid row hotels
    B. Middle-class hotels
    C. Working-class hotels
    D. all of the above

15. About _____ of U.S. individuals over age 65 reside in an institution.
    A. 5%
    B. 15%
    C. 25%
    D. 35%

16. The typical nursing home patient is
    A. a minority.
    B. financially well off.
    C. a woman.
    D. all of the above

17. Bernstein found that housing project tenants were commonly asked to leave for all of the following reasons **except** when they
    A. showed mental decline.
    B. had alcohol problems.
    C. did not pay the rent.
    D. were a safety hazard to themselves and others.

18. Harel found that the best predictor of congruence in a nursing home setting was a residents ability to
    A. identify the regulations of the home.
    B. continue ties with a selected member of his or her social network.
    C. afford the best care available.
    D. select their own in-home nurse.

19. Moos's Multiphasic Environmental Assessment Procedure (MEAP) assesses the _____ characteristics of an institution.
    A. physical
    B. social
    C. administrative
    D. all of the above

20. A nursing home with rules against married couples engaging in sexual activity would create a _____ based congruence problem for a couple who had an active sex life before they entered the home.
    A. impulse-control   C. congregate
    B. affect   D. stimulation-engagement

21. In recent years, the population of Arizona and Florida have been significantly increased because of
    A. amenity mobility   C. kinship mobility
    B. widowhood mobility   D. generational mobility

22. _____ appears to be an important variable in the ability of someone to adjust to a move.
    A. Distance of the move
    B. Amount of attachment to the old home
    C. Voluntary nature of the move
    D. all of the above

23. Research has shown that survival among nursing home patients is related to all of the following personality traits **except**
    A. hostility.   C. acceptance.
    B. aggression.   D. narcissism.

24. Which statement concerning relocation and adjustment is **false**?
    A. Relocation has a direct effect on mortality.
    B. Appropriateness of the new facility is important.
    C. The nature of relocation (voluntary versus involuntary) is critical.
    D. Individuals how do not normally handle stress well are especially affected by relocation.

III. SHORT-ANSWER ESSAY (QUESTIONS AND ANSWERS)

Questions

1. Describe Lewin's person-environment interaction equation.

2. Identify the three conditions Kahana proposed that can limit a person's behavior.

3. Briefly summarize the results from Krout's study of community size and awareness for services.

4. Differentiate among retirement communities, congregate housing, and continuing care retirement communities.

5. Discuss Erickson and Ekert's types of SRO hotels.

6. Differentiate among nursing homes, personal-care homes, boarding homes, and psychiatric hospitals.

7. What is the average cost of nursing home care and how is it financed?

8. Identify and briefly describe Kahana's seven environmental and individual dimensions of congruence. Be sure to provide an example of each type.

9. Discuss the common failings of nursing homes proposed by Langer.

10. Describe Speare and Meyer's types of mobility.

11. Discuss factors that appear to affect a person's ability to adjust to a move.

Answers

1. Lewin's person-environment equation was $B = f(P,E)$ where B = behavior, P = the person, and E = the environment. Lewin argued that a person's behavior is a function of the interaction between a person and the world around him or her. (p. 412)

2. According to Kahana's congruence model, individuals may be limited for any of the following reasons: (a) They reside in a restricted environment. (b) They truly have limited freedom to act. (c) They believe they have limited freedom to act. (p. 415)

3. Krout utilized survey and interview techniques to investigate the relationship between community size and awareness by elderly people for available social services. He found that awareness varied by (a) predisposition factors (e.g., age, gender race, marital status); (b) enabling factors (e.g., income, transportation availability); (c) need factor (e.g., health conditions); and (d) community size (people in larger communities were more aware of services). (p. 419)

4. Retirement communities are areas designed to cater to the needs of an elderly population. They can include specific housing, transportation, and shopping services. Congregate housing involves individual housing units designed as an intermediate step between independent living and institutionalization. These housing units may contain several apartments all linked to a central office that handles emergencies. Continuing care retirement communities include a number of different types of living arrangements ranging from complete independence to full nursing home care. Individuals move from one type of housing unit to another depending on need. (p. 423-425)

5. SRO (single-room-occupancy) housing offer a hotel-like alternative living arrangement for older adults. These structures are often found in inner city locations and have been classified by Erickson and Ekert into the following three types: (a) skid row (deteriorated with mostly low-income tenants); (b) working-class (relatively clean units with house keeping service available); and (c) middle-income (more comfortable and expensive units). (p. 424)

6. Nursing homes are residential care facilities that provide housing and medical care services to their clients. The two types of federally funded nursing care facilities are skilled nursing facilities (providing 24-hour medical care) and intermediate nursing facilities (providing nursing supervision and less intense care). Personal-care and boarding homes are small units often designed to assist people with chronic movement-related disorders (e.g., arthritis). Psychiatric hospitals provide care for individuals with severe psychological disorders. (p. 427)

7. In 1990, the average cost of nursing home care was $25,000 per year. This cost is typically pay for by individuals who are often forced to deplete their savings and sell off their belongings before Medicaid takes over the payments. (p. 428)

8. Kahana identified the following key congruence dimensions: (a) segregate (environment--presence of daily routine, individual--preference for daily variety); (b) congregate (environment--availability of privacy, individual--need for privacy); (c) institutional control (environment--amount of deviance tolerated, individual--need to conform); (d) structure (environment--specification of rules, individual--need for structure); (e) stimulation-engagement (environment--extent to which an individual is encouraged to be active, individual--preference for activity); (f) affect (environment--tolerance for displays of affection, individual--need for emotional expression); and (g) impulse control (environment--tolerance for motor expression, individual--motor control). (p. 432-433)

9. Langer believed that nursing homes use many practices that lead to a loss of perceived control by residents. The detrimental practices include: (a) Staff members may indicate the belief that the patient is incapable of making a logical decision. (b) The label "nursing home patient" may lead to stereotypic treatment. (c) Demonstrations of assistance (e.g., helping someone dress) may reinforce beliefs of incompetence. (d) The physical environment may reinforce the perceived lack of control. (e) A strict routine may promote "mindlessness." (p. 434)

10. Speare and Meyer proposed that older people move because of (a) amenity mobility (climate reasons); (b) kinship mobility (family closeness); (c) retirement mobility; and (d) widowhood mobility (social support systems other than family members). (p. 435)

11. Several factors appear to be critical in an individual's ability to adjust to a move. Some of these factors include (a) social status (people with higher educations and socioeconomic status appear to adjust better); (b) social support systems (individuals with strong support systems adjust better); (c) environmental factors (location and physical structure of new dwelling can be critical); and (d) perception of the move (the belief in control over the move can reduce anxiety). (p. 437-438)

IV. AFTER THE FACTS

1. Think about the perfect city, neighborhood, and house? Do you think that you have a chance to live in any such locations?

2. What would be the hardest part of residing in a nursing home? Would there be any benefits?

3. Speculate on future housing/health facility options (aimed at the large number of elderly persons expected early next century).

4. Can you draw any parallels between your college-life moves (too college and around campus) and the information on adjustment to moves and relocation discussed in the text?

V. REVIEW ANSWERS

Terms to Know
Check the Key Terms section for Chapter 12 (p. 443)

True/False Answers
1. False (p.414)	6. False (p.425)
2. True (p.416)	7. True (p.427)
3. False (p.417)	8. False (p.429)
4. False (p.420)	9. False (p.436)
5. True (p.421)	10. True (p.437)

Fill-in-the-Blank(s) Answers
1. Environmental (p. 411)
2. Competence (p. 413)
3. social support systems (p. 416)
4. informal social network (p. 417)
5. church (p. 421)
6. participant observation (p. 422)
7. person-environment (p. 426)
8. health (p. 429)
9. perceive themselves in control of their lives (p. 431)
10. physical surroundings (p. 438)

Multiple Choice Answers
1. D (p.412)	9. A (p.420)	17. C (p.430)
2. B (p.412)	10. A (p.421)	18. B (p.430-431)
3. D (p.413)	11. D (p.422-423)	19. D (p.431)
4. A (p.413)	12. A (p.423-424)	20. B (p.432-433)
5. D (p.413-414)	13. B (p.423-424)	21. A (p.435)
6. D (p.416)	14. B (p.424)	22. D (p.437)
7. C (p.417-418)	15. A (p.426)	23. C (p.439)
8. B (p.418)	16. C (p.427)	24. A (p.440-441)

CHAPTER 13
DYING AND BEREAVEMENT

I. PREVIEW

Focus Questions

☞ **How is death defined?**
(Focus on: Sociocultural Definitions of Death; Legal and Medical Definitions)

☞ **Why is euthanasia such a controversial topic?**
(Focus on: Ethical Issues; Something to Think About: Bioethics, Euthanasia, and Controversy)

☞ **What causes death anxiety?**
(Focus on: Death Anxiety)

☞ **How do people react when told they are dying?**
(Focus on: The Stage Theory of Dying; The Phase Theory of Dying)

☞ **What is the basic premise of a hospice?**
(Focus on: The Hospice Alternative)

☞ **How do normal and abnormal grieving differ?**
(Focus on: Stages of Grief; Normal Grief Reactions; Abnormal Grief Reactions)

☞ **Are certain types of loss more difficult than others?**
(Focus on: Types of Loss and Grieving)

Chapter 13: DYING AND BEREAVEMENT

Chapter Outline

Special Sections
Something to Think About
How Do We Know?

II. REVIEW

Terms to Know
Write your own brief definition for each of the following terms.

Anniversary Reaction:

Brain Death:

Clinical Death:

Cortical Death:

Dying Trajectory:

Euthanasia:

Grief Work:

Hospice:

Near-Death Experience:

True/False Questions

____ 1. Americans tend to be fascinated by the death of others but terrified by their own deaths.

____ 2. Younger people are more likely to think about death on an everyday basis.

____ 3. Cortical death can occur even if there is functioning within the brainstem.

____ 4. Death anxiety may be related to your occupation.

___ 5. According to Kübler-Ross, when people are told they have a terminal illness their first reaction is anger.

___ 6. Older persons are more likely to die in isolation.

___ 7. In the U.S., about 75 percent of people die in a hospital or nursing home.

___ 8. Most terminally ill patients would rather not be told they are dying.

___ 9. An expected death tends to produce less psychological trauma.

___ 10. The key difference between normal and abnormal grief involves the intensity and duration of a person's reactions.

Fill-in-the-Blank(s) Questions

1. Melanesians use the term mate when referring to the very sick, the very old or the _____.

2. A _____ of death is founded on the premise that we believe we have been allotted a specific amount of years of life and feel cheated if we die "before our time."

3. Clinical death is defined as the lack of _____.

4. _____ is the study of the interface between human values and technological advances in heath and life sciences.

5. The emotion of _____ underlies all components of death anxiety.

6. The term _____ is used to describe the length and form of a person's dying process.

7. The best predictor of nursing home admission is _____.

8. The phrase _____ is used to describe a situation in which both a patient and family members know a patient is dying but everyone acts as if the condition is not serious.

9. _____ refers to the ways in which we express our grief.

10. Feelings of sadness experienced on the birthday of a person who died ten-years ago reflect a(n) _____ reaction.

Chapter 13: DYING AND BEREAVEMENT

Multiple Choice Questions

1. The moral of the Buddhist Parable of the Mustard Seed is
   A. life is impermanent.
   B. death is bitter.
   C. new life springs from old.
   D. there is a garden in the afterlife.

2. A flag at half staff fits into the _____ view of death.
   A. image
   B. analogy
   C. state of being
   D. boundary

3. The concept of heaven may be found in all of the following death views **except**
   A. reward and punishment.
   B. boundary
   C. a state of being.
   D. as robbed of the meaning of life.

4. Dr. Jack Kevorkian's "the suicide doctor" use of a machine to induce death represents an example of _____ euthanasia.
   A. voluntary (requested by the patient) active
   B. involuntary (not requested by the patient) active
   C. voluntary (requested by the patient) passive
   D. involuntary (requested by the patient) passive

5. Which is **not** typically found in a living will?
   A. wishes concerning the use of life support systems
   B. the name of a specific person with legal authority to speak for you
   C. a statement concerning possible surgical measures to be taken if you are in an accident
   D. all of the above

6. The Dutch Supreme Court recently eliminated prosecution for physicians who assist in suicide if certain criteria are met. Which is **not** one of the criteria?
   A. The patient must make the request several times.
   B. The patient must be incompetent.
   C. Two physicians must agree with the patient's request.
   D. The patient's condition must be intolerable with no hope for improvement.

7. Most individuals in Western societies agree that extraordinary efforts should be made to save all
   A. premature infants.
   B. terminally ill older persons.
   C. AIDS patients.
   D. all of the above

8. Research on death anxiety has found that
   A. men are more anxious about death than are women.
   B. people with strong religious convictions do not fear death.
   C. elderly people appear to be less fearful of death than do younger people.
   D. all of the above

9. A benefit to death anxiety appears to be that it
   A. strengthens one's desire to live.
   B. may help motivate us to raise children better.
   C. helps ensure the survival of the species.
   D. all of the above

10. Which is a way to show death anxiety?
    A. being a fire fighter   C. avoiding a funeral
    B. being a mortician   D. all of the above

Chapter 13: DYING AND BEREAVEMENT

11. Kübler-Ross's _____ stage is characterized by the feeling that death is "unfair."
    A. denial   C. depression
    B. anger   D. bargaining

12. Death anxiety appears highest when death is
    A. certain and the length of time until death is known.
    B. certain but the length of time until death is unknown.
    C. uncertain but will be clear in a specific amount of time.
    D. all of the above

13. Ambiguity lengthens the _____ phase of dying.
    A. acute-crisis   C. living-dying
    B. chronic   D. terminal

14. One difference between the death of old versus young people is that
    A. financial costs are greater for older people.
    B. younger people have more of an opportunity to visit old friends.
    C. older people have less time to plan for their deaths.
    D. younger people have more potential for leading a normal life during the early phases of the dying process.

15. The institutionalization of death has resulted in all of the following **except**
    A. an increase in death anxiety.
    B. an increase in personal contact with death.
    C. an increase in the role of health care workers in death.
    D. an increase in the ethical dilemma of life versus death facing medical staffs.

16. Which is **not** a basic premise of hospices?
    A. keeping a patient free from pain even if it means administering drugs
    B. involving family members in the process as much as possible
    C. discouraging clients from severing relationships
    D. trying to alleviate fear

17. _____ is a primary need for all dying persons.
    A. Relief from pain
    B. Retention of dignity and self-worth
    C. Love and affection from others
    D. all of the above

18. In the past,
    A. physicians saw the death of a patient as a personal failure.
    B. physicians tended to seekout patients who they found out were dying.
    C. nurses responded quicker to call lights from terminal patients.
    D. all of the above

19. Which is **not** an example of mourning?
    A. wearing white clothing
    B. marrying the deceased spouse's sibling
    C. attending a funeral
    D. feeling sad about the loss of the deceased

20. Which is common of a person in the intermediate phase of grief?
    A. improved self-confidence
    B. dreams of conversing with the deceased
    C. confusion
    D. feelings of the inability to continue one's life

21. Kalish stated that the most common source of guilt is the result of the _____ syndrome.
    A. "We"   C. "If only I had"
    B. "It should have been me"   D. "It can't happen to me"

22. The most common grief reaction involves
    A. sadness.   C. loneliness.
    B. fear.   D. anger.

23. Perkins and Harris found that _____ people were most likely to report physical health problems following the death of a spouse, sibling, or sibling-in-law.
    A. young   C. old
    B. middle-age

24. Research on the death of a loved one has shown that
    A. the loss of a parent is not as significant if it occurs when the surviving child is middle-aged.
    B. parents recover quickly from a neonatal death.
    C. bereaved spouses tend to rate their marriage as more satisfactory than nonbereaved spouses.
    D. older adults tend to shown a more intense reaction immediately following the death of their spouse.

III. SHORT-ANSWER ESSAY (QUESTIONS AND ANSWERS)

Questions

1. Identify the various ways that Kalish and Kastenbaum thought death could be viewed.

2. List the current criteria for brain death.

3. Differentiate between active and passive euthanasia.

4. Identify Shulz's components of death anxiety.

5. Describe different ways of showing death anxiety.

6. Discuss Kübler-Ross's stage theory of dying.

7. Briefly describe Pattison's phase theory of dying.

8. List Kalish's six factors for determining where a person will die.

9. Describe the three phases of grief.

10. Summarize the major findings from Norris and Murrell's study of bereavement and family stress.

11. List common aspects of reports by persons having a near-death experience.

Answers

1. Kalish and Kastenbaum thought that death could be viewed as any of the following: (a) an image--a visual reminder of death (e.g., tombstone); (b) a statistic--in terms of numbers (e.g., mortality rates); (c) an event--a ceremony with legal implications (e.g., funeral); (d) a state of being--another type of "life" (e.g., heaven); (e) an analogy--an example to convey uselessness (e.g., "the batteries dead"); (f) the ultimate mystery; (g) a boundary--an endpoint of earthly existence; (h) a thief of meaning--something that robs us of our earthly pleasures; (i) a basis for fear or anxiety; and (j) a reward or punishment for our earthly behaviors (e.g., heaven or hell). (p. 448-449)

2. The criteria for brain death include (a) no spontaneous movement in response to any stimuli; (b) no spontaneous respiration for at least 1 hour; (c) lack of responsiveness to painful stimuli; (d) no eye movement or pupil response; (e) no postural or verbal activity; (f) no motor reflexes; (g) a flat electroencephalogram for at least 10 minutes; and (h) no change in any of the afore mentioned criteria when tested 24 hours later. (p. 450)

3. Euthanasia is the practice of ending a person's life for reasons of mercy. Active euthanasia involves a deliberate act taken to end a persons life (e.g., administering a drug). Passive euthanasia involves causing a death by withholding treatment (e.g., do not perform surgery that may prolong life). Because the distinction between the types of euthanasia is so vague, many people have a difficult time forming an opinion concerning the morality of the act. (p. 451-452)

4. Schulz believed that death anxiety was composed of of several components including: (a) pain; (b) body malfunction; (c) humiliation; (d) rejection; (e) nonbeing; (f) punishment; (g) interruption of goals; and (h) negative impact of survivors. In addition, we may respond differently to death at public (what we show others), private (what we feel when we are alone), and nonconscious (internal beliefs that are hard to access) levels. (p. 454)

5. People demonstrate death anxiety in many ways. Some avoid all situations dealing with death (e.g., do not attend funeral visitations). Some engage in occupations or hobbies that challenge death (e.g., soldier, skydiver). Others deal with anxiety by dreaming about death, laughing about death, or taking up an occupation that deals directly with death (e.g., ambulance driver, mortician). (p. 455-456)

6. Kübler-Ross believed that individuals tend to follow a five-stage sequence when dealing with their own deaths: (a) denial (the belief that a mistake has been made and they are not going to die); (b) anger (hostility an resentment toward the living); (c) bargaining (striking a deal to prolong life, typically with some supreme being); (d) depression (including sorrow, shame, guilt); and (e) acceptance (accepting the inevitability of death an beginning to detach from the world of the living). (p. 456-457)

7. Pattison saw death as progressing through three phases: (a) acute crisis (begins when a person is made aware of impending death--marked by high anxiety, denial, anger); (b) chronic living dying (begins when a person starts to deal with emotions associated with impending death--marked by loneliness, fear of the unknown, grief); and (c) terminal (begins when a person accepts death--marked by a withdrawal from the world). (p. 457-458)

8. Kalish identified the following factors as predictors of where death will take place: (a) physical condition; (b) availability of care; (c) financial status; (d) competence of institutional personnel; (e) age; and (f) personal preferences. (p. 460)

9. Most researchers divide the grieving process into the following phases: (a) initial (from notification of death through several weeks--characterized by shock, disbelief, sadness); (b) intermediate (characterized by obsessive thought concerning the deceased, guilt, a feeling of the "presence" of the deceased, an attempt to understand why the person died); and (c) recovery (a conscious decision to move on with one's life--characterized by increased social activity and improved self-confidence). (p. 467)

10. The two major findings from the Norris and Murrell study of
family stress and bereavement were: (a) The level of stress
experienced by bereaved families were higher than nonbereaved
families prior to the person's death, peaked during the death
interval, and returned to a normal levels after about one year.
(b) Bereavement had little effect on physical health. (p. 470-473)

11. Common reports given by people having had near-death
experiences include (a) hearing sounds including the
pronouncement of one's own death; (b) feeling of movement down a
tunnel or toward a light; (c) seeing or feeling the presence of a dead
relative; (d) sensing a power that causes one to review one's life;
(e) viewing one's own life passing in front of one's eyes; (f) having
instant access to any knowledge; and (g) being aware that one's time
is "not up" and feeling the need to return to finish one's life on earth.
(p.   475-476)

IV. AFTER THE FACTS

1. Are you anxious about death? If so, which aspects produce the most anxiety? Can you think of ways to reduce this anxiety?

2. How do you think that you would react if you found out tomorrow that you had a terminal illness? How would you want those around you to react?

3. What types of future losses do you think will have the most impact on you? Are there ways to reduce the impact?

4. Will scientists be able to determine if there is life after death? What kind of "proof" would they need to convince you?

Chapter 13: DYING AND BEREAVEMENT

V. REVIEW ANSWERS

Terms to Know
Check the Key Terms section for Chapter 13 (p. 479)

True/False Answers
1. True (p.446)   6. True (p.459)
2. False (p.449)   7. True (p.459)
3. True (p.451)   8. False (p.464)
4. True (p.455)   9. True (p.465-466)
5. False (p.456-457) 10. True (p.471)

Fill-in-the-Blank(s) Answers
1. dead (p. 477)
2. just world view (p. 449)
3. a heartbeat and respiration (p. 449-450)
4. Bioethics (p. 451)
5. fear (p. 454)
6. death trajectory (p. 457)
7. degree of available social support (p. 460)
8. mutual pretense (p. 464)
9. mourning (p. 465)
10. anniversary (p. 470)

Multiple Choice Answers
1. A (p.446)   9. D (p.455)   17. D (p.462-463)
2. A (p.448-449) 10. D (p.455-456) 18. A (p.463)
3. D (p.448-449) 11. B (p.457)   19. D (p.465)
4. A (p.451-452) 12. C (p.457-458) 20. B (p.467)
5. B (p.451-452) 13. A (p.458)   21. C (p.469)
6. B (p.452)   14. A (p.459)   22. A (p.469)
7. A (p.452-453) 15. B (p.459-460) 23. B (p.470)
8. C (p.454-455) 16. C (p.461)   24. C (p.474-475)

CHAPTER 14
LOOKING TOWARD THE 21ST CENTURY

I. PREVIEW

Focus Questions

☞ **How can we improve research on aging?**
(Focus on: The Need for Better Research)

☞ **What demographic changes are likely to occur in the U.S. in the next forty years?**
(Focus on: Changing Demographics)

☞ **Why are health care issues expected to become more important in the near future?**
(Focus on: Health Care)

☞ **How can we make later life more productive?**
(Focus on: Productive Roles for Older Adults)

Chapter 14: LOOKING TOWARD THE 21ST CENTURY

Chapter Outline

II. REVIEW

True/False Questions

____ 1. The elderly population in the U.S. will double by the year 2030.

____ 2. For-profit health care organizations tend to have highly structured recovery programs for different age groups.

____ 3. The National Research Center recommended against increasing the amount of money spent on health promotion and disease prevention.

____ 4. Living past one's expected time of death may create psychological anxiety.

____ 5. If scientists are able to extend the lifespan, age-related health care problems would likely be eliminated.

Fill-in-the-Blank(s) Questions

1. _____ research designs can assess cohort effects.

2. The National Research Center identified the _____ as the most important health issue facing the U.S. in the 1990s.

3. In _____ aging, external factors intensify the effects of physiological processes, whereas in _____ aging, external factors play a neutral or positive role.

4. The Committee on an Aging Society views _____ roles as one way to ensure future significant societal contributions by older persons.

5. It is likely that in the near future, the focus on cognitive research will shift to how adults think on _____.

Chapter 14: LOOKING TOWARD THE 21ST CENTURY

Multiple Choice Questions

1. Which is **not** one of the gerontological "future crises" identified in your text?
   A. the need for better research
   B. health care and related issues
   C. the population explosion
   D. the need to create a more productive role for the elderly

2. To be more effective, aging researchers need to limit or eliminate the use of _____ research designs.
   A. longitudinal   C. sequential
   B. cross-sectional   D. all of the above

3. Which statement concerning future research is **false**?
   A. There needs to be more interdisciplinary work between cognitive and neurological scientists.
   B. Researchers need to realize that intellectual needs may change from generation to generation.
   C. Researchers need to change research priorities from a focus on quality to a focus on quantity.
   D. Researchers need to determine whether age-related differences are innate or related to history effects.

4. By the year 2030, the ratio of workers to retirees will be about
   A. 20:1.   C. 2:1.
   B. 10:1.   D. 1:1.

5. Which of the following is expected to happen by the year 2030?
   A. Middle-age adults may feel less obligated to their parents.
   B. Older adults will expect to keep more of their social security benefits.
   C. Older adults will become more politically organized and active.
   D. all of the above

6. By the year 2000, the over-80 age group will be receiving more than _____ a year in federal entitlement benefits.
   A. $80 million
   B. $800 million
   C. $8 billion
   D. $80 billion

7. The author of the text indicated that the most important contribution of psychology to the study of aging involves the
   A. identification of the cause of cancer.
   B. demonstration that declines in psychological functioning are not an inevitable part of aging.
   C. demonstration of the lack of individual variations in aging.
   D. all of the above

8. Golant hypothesized that the 21st century will see a spotlight on
   A. MUPPIES (minority urban professionals).
   B. DINKS (double income–no kids).
   C. YEEPIES (youthful energetic elderly people involved in everything).
   D. MIMIES (middle-age, middle-income individuals).

9. Older adults participate in unpaid volunteer activities
   A. significantly more often than young or middle-age individuals.
   B. significantly less often than young or middle-age individuals.
   C. at about the same rate as young or middle-age individuals.

10. _____ disease is thought by many to mirror the qualitative changes found in normal aging.
    A. Alzheimer's
    B. Pick's
    C. Huntington's
    D. Parkinson's

III. SHORT-ANSWER ESSAY (QUESTIONS AND ANSWERS)

Questions

1. Discuss the major demographic and related changes predicted for the year 2030.

2. Describe the recommendations concerning future health care proposed by the National Research Council.

3. Identify methods that can be used to eliminate barriers to volunteerism by elderly individuals.

Answers

1. Predictions for changes related to demographics by the year 2030 include (a) a doubling of the elderly population; (b) a more organized and political elderly population; (c) higher expectations among older people concerning entitlement benefits; (d) a decrease in the worker-to-retiree ratio to around 2:1; (e) increased conflict between middle- and old-age generations; and (f) a rapid increase in the elderly minority population. (p. 483)

2. The National Research Council made the following recommendations concerning health care for the elderly: (a) Address the way health care is funded (e.g., reduce out-of-pocket costs paid by individuals). (b) Change the health care delivery system (e.g., increase availability to rural and inner-city residents). (c) Promote disease prevention. (p. 484)

3. Barriers to volunteerism of older adults could be eliminated in several ways including: (a) explicitly recognizing the unique skills and wealth of information of the elderly; (b) making specific appeals to older adults to get involved and share their knowledge; (c) increasing incentives for volunteering; (d) improving the organization of volunteer programs; and (e) providing transportation. (p. 488-489)

IV. AFTER THE FACTS

1. Which of the expected demographic changes will have the greatest impact on U.S. society? What steps might be taken to reduce this expected crisis?

2. Can the Social Security/Medicare system handle our future retirement and health concerns? What alternatives to this system do you expect to hear about in the next 20 years?

3. How has the information you acquired by reading this text changed the way you think about aging and adult development? What were the most surprising new "facts" you encountered? Which existing ideas were supported?

V. REVIEW ANSWERS

True/False Answers
1. True (p.483)
2. False (p.484)
3. False (p.484)
4. True (p.486)
5. False (p.489-490)

Fill-in-the-Blank(s) Answers
1. Sequential (p. 482)
2. financing of medical care for the elderly (p. 484)
3. "usual" (p. 486); "successful" (p. 486)
4. unpaid productive (p. 488)
5. everyday applied problems (p. 490)

Multiple Choice answers:
1. C (p.481-482)
2. B (p.482-483)
3. C (p.482-483)
4. C (p.483)
5. D (p.483)
6. D (p.484)
7. B (p.485-486)
8. C (p.487)
9. C (p.487)
10. A (p.489)